SUCCESS WITH
BANDSAWS

SUCCESS WITH
BANDSAWS

ERIC GRAVES

TECHNICAL ADVISER: ANTHONY BAILEY
STAFF WRITER: MICHAEL BURTON

GUILD OF MASTER CRAFTSMAN PUBLICATIONS LTD

First published 2007 by
Guild of Master Craftsman Publications Ltd
Castle Place, 166 High Street
Lewes, East Sussex BN7 1XU

Technical Adviser: Anthony Bailey
Staff Writer: Michael Burton

ISBN-13: 978-1-86108-473-6
ISBN-10: 1-86108-473-0

A catalogue record for this book is available from the British Library.

Production Manager: Jim Bulley
Managing Editor: Gerrie Purcell
Project Editor: Gill Parris
Chief Photographer: Anthony Bailey © GMC Publications Ltd,
with the following exceptions:
Record Power, p. 12 left, p. 13 left, p. 22, p. 24, p. 27, p. 29,
p. 33 right and p. 34 top)
Grizzly Industrial Inc. (p. 15 middle left).
Managing Art Editor: Gilda Pacitti
Designer: John Hawkins

Set in Frutiger and Palatino
Colour origination by MRM Graphics
Printed and bound by Sino Publishing, China

Contents

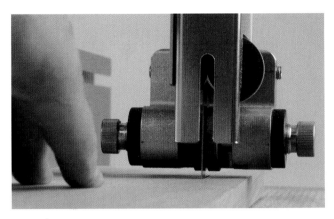

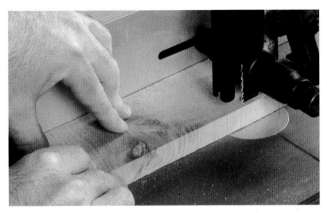

Introduction

Bandsaws cut wood effectively in a wide variety of ways. Their simplicity allows for rapidly pleasing results, yet permits you to develop both the machine's and your own potential for far greater rewards. Learning to use the bandsaw competently is one of the most satisfying undertakings for a woodworker.

By comparison with most woodworking machines the bandsaw is both straightforward to use and relatively user-friendly. It requires a much more hands-on approach, giving the user an intimacy rarely experienced with other machines. This should not fool the novice user into thinking safety is not an issue here; care is required just as much with a bandsaw as with any other machine.

The bandsaw is comparatively safe to use and is a good deal quieter than many of its companions in the workshop. This makes it easier to work with for longer periods of time, as excessive noise in confined spaces can add significantly to operator fatigue. Finally, and critically, it is highly versatile and capable of a wide range of operations on various materials. Once a few basic skills have been acquired, any number of projects can be tackled.

This book deals with bandsaws in relation to woodworking only, but it should be noted that bandsaws work equally effectively for other materials, including metals and plastics. We start with an examination of the essential components, including bandsaw blades – and proceed to a general overview of the bandsaw and what can be achieved with it: setting-up procedures, machine maintenance, health and safety issues, uses and abuses, and the all-important techniques and cutting jigs.

With correct care and attention, there is no good reason why you and your bandsaw should not be perfect workmates in a long and fruitful partnership, and I wish you the best of luck in your woodworking endeavours.

Part 1:
The Bandsaw

1:1 What is a bandsaw?

In 1809 William Newberry patented a looped blade rotating on two wheels, one above the other, thus creating a continuous sawing action. This is much like the bandsaw of today, and it remains a design classic. The modern version has many innovations, including vital safety features missing from the original design, but it is still recognizably the same basic machine in a modern guise.

A bandsaw consists of a motorized set of two rotating wheels (three-wheeled models are no longer common) holding a flexible saw blade under tension, thus allowing for the continuous cutting of a variety of materials which are supported on its table. The blade is totally enclosed, except for a vertical working section between the top saw guide and the table, which is exposed for the actual cutting process. The downward motion of the blade helps to keep the workpiece flat to the table.

Using a bandsaw is not unlike working with the lathe, in that much of the control required is in the fingertips – but it is not as difficult to master. A well-tuned bandsaw can be a real pleasure to use, as opposed to the sometimes rather mechanical and repetitive exercise of cutting or shaping material with other workshop machinery.

The bandsaw is capable of precision work, whether cutting curves, circles or straight lines, thick or thin timber, cutting boards from logs, even cutting veneers – indeed anything from fine furniture joints to jigsaw puzzles. Because of this it is an indispensable addition to any serious woodworking venture and, consequently, the popular choice for many woodworkers as their first machine. It also has a small workshop footprint, which makes it a good choice when space is limited.

Bandsaw types

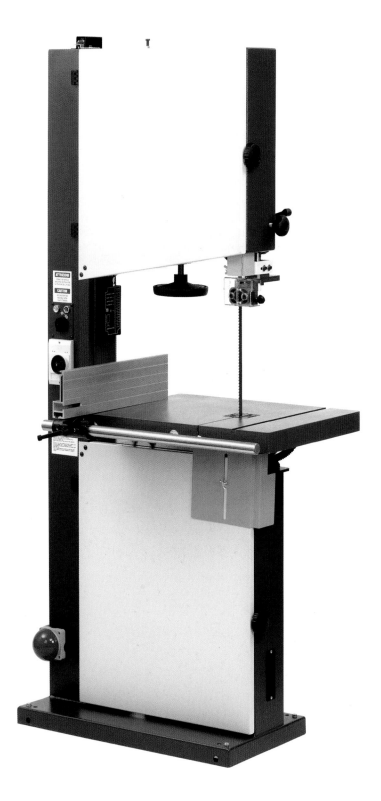

Bandsaws are generally classified firstly according to their build, which falls into one of three categories:

• floor models
• stand-mounted saws
• bench-top saws

The **floor models** are the larger, industrial saws with big wheels contained in large cabinets which rest directly on the floor.

Stand-mounted saws are mounted on their own stand, which is separate from the main machine and often houses the motor and drive belt. They have more weight, size and power than the ordinary bench style of bandsaw.

Bench-top saws, which rest on a workbench or table top, are smaller and more compact, even to the point of being portable in some cases. However, generally speaking, what you gain in portability you lose in power.

LEFT This sturdy, well-built floor-standing model is capable of industrial-grade work.

ABOVE A good-quality, medium-size, stand-mounted machine, suitable for a domestic or trade workshop.

ABOVE A low-cost, compact, bench-top machine.

A bandsaw with large-diameter bandwheels, or a three-wheel bandsaw, will have a greater throat width, allowing for a larger table and greater working area.

Another figure which may be referred to is the depth of cut available – distance between the table top and the apex of the usable part of the saw blade under the top guides, which determines the maximum depth of cut achievable. This figure is often between 6in (152mm) and 8in (200mm) on more 'domestic' models, but is significantly more on the higher-grade industrial machines.

ABOVE This machine has considerable width (or throat) capacity, which extends beyond the table to the case column.

Some US models feature an extra component called a 'riser block', which can be inserted into the column post. This can, effectively, add up to 6in (152mm) to the depth of cut.

The apparent simplicity of the bandsaw and its components belies the complex interrelationship these constituent parts have to one another. Like all other pieces of workshop machinery, for truly effective use the bandsaw must be correctly set up and finely tuned. Carrying out this process will acquaint you with your machine, thus giving you valuable knowledge and insight into its functioning parts and its capabilities; it will also instil more confidence once you do begin work with it. From then on in it is a matter of honing your skills in order to bring out the best from both yourself and your machine.

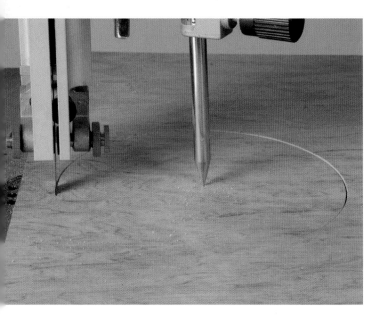

ABOVE Even a simple operation, such as cutting out circles from square board, can be hampered by the presence of the column if your machine has insufficient throat width.

A second important consideration is the width of the throat, that distance between the blade and the upright column connecting the upper and lower wheel chambers: a 14in (356mm) bandsaw is described as a machine with a throat width of 14in (356mm).

The capabilities of the bandsaw are brought about primarily through the blades employed and, by using blades of different widths, the versatility of the saw is greatly extended. With a $\frac{1}{16}$in (2mm) blade, intricate shaping of wood (known as intarsia), or the delicate manipulation of veneers (known as marquetry), can be carried out.

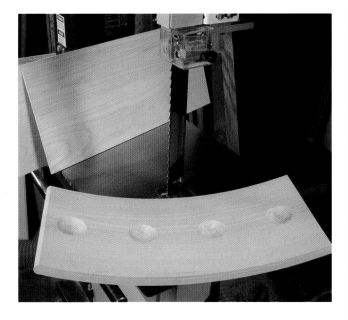

ABOVE Cutting wide components, such as this base for an unusual stand mirror, requires plenty of height under the upper guides.

ABOVE This cast-iron riser-block kit features the block-tensioning bars, bolt, extended guard and, of course, a longer blade.

At the other extreme, using a ¾in (19mm) blade, resawing (the cutting down of thick stock into thinner boards or strips) is easily achievable. Using this technique veneers can be cut and, by using woods with interesting grain structures – often the more expensive and exotic hardwoods – highly decorative finishes are possible, where the use of solid timber would be prohibitively expensive. The bandsaw is also the ideal machine for sawing complex exterior curves on a range of materials, from solid wood to composite boards and even metal sheets.

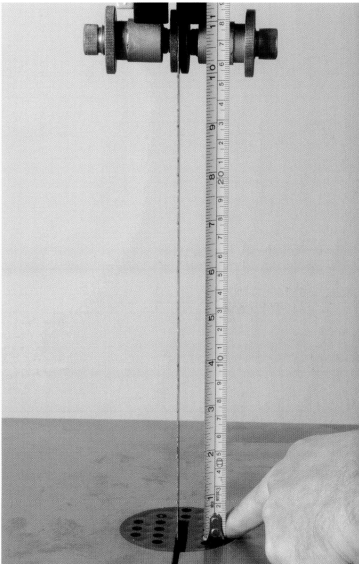

ABOVE Checking with a tape measure to ascertain the true height under the guides. As long as the workpiece is parallel in cut height from top to bottom, you can use the maximum capacity of your machine.

⊙KEY POINT

Wherever possible, use timber stock from renewable sources. Ask your timber merchant about this, or use specific companies who deal in ecologically friendly resources (see 'Resources', on page 170).

Basic functions

The bandsaw can carry out a host of functions otherwise performed by individual pieces of machinery, thus saving a great deal of time and energy:

• **It can rip like a tablesaw**, but remove far less stock and with less resistance, and so less power is needed to perform the cut; there is, therefore, also less chance of disfiguring the timber with burn marks, which is a consequence of a saw blade heating up due to

the friction caused during cutting, a situation often associated with tablesaw blades. Because the workpiece is effectively being forced down onto the saw table by the continuous downward pressure of the blade, another bonus is that there is no chance of it being thrown up and out at the operator. This situation, known as 'kickback', is unfortunately a common occurrence with tablesaws, accounting for many accidents in the workshop and on site.

RIGHT Ripping down boards is quick and easy with little waste. In this case a cupped board is being divided, resulting in two much flatter, narrow boards.

• **It can cut out joints like a handsaw**, including the classical joints used by the woodworker, such as tenons (used for constructing frames in door-making or case work, or for joining legs to rails on tables and chairs); dovetails (as used in the strong, yet decorative, joining of drawer sides), and lap joints (often used in carpentry work). These are all achievable with reasonable ease, using a correctly set up bandsaw with the right blade. These joints can be both pleasing on the eye and have great mechanical strength, while providing large gluing areas for added strength.

• **It can follow patterns as a bearing-guided router would**, so that efficient reproduction of shaped pieces can be carried out rapidly and effectively. This is achieved by butting up a guide stick to the blade – set to marry up to a template fixed to the workpiece with double-sided tape or small brads. Multiples can then be produced time and again with ease. The final result will lack the precision finish possible with a router, but the finish will certainly be reasonable, and it will have saved an enormous amount of time as compared to cutting pieces individually marked out.

ABOVE Many cabinetmakers favour the bandsaw for cutting dovetails – skill is involved and satisfaction, too.

BELOW It is possible to follow a variably curved edge, with a bandsaw, as shown here.

(FOCUS ON:

Basic functions

ABOVE Here two cuts are about to meet. It is often better to cut from more than one direction when curves may be tight and difficult to follow.

- **It can cut intricate shapes like a scrollsaw or jigsaw**, with the advantage of continual downward blade motion, pushing the work against the table. The reciprocating motion of a jigsaw or scrollsaw may cause greater workpiece movement. Greater concentration and focus is possible with the bandsaw, making those trickier cuts easier to perform (with the correct blade, of course).

- **The bandsaw can cut compound curves easily** The ability to cut compound curves – that is, working to a curved line with the table set to an angle to produce a bevelled curve – is made possible because the table on a bandsaw is invariably capable of tilting. This angle setting can be repeated at any time, thanks to a protractor scale which allows you to reset it precisely.

ABOVE Simply tilting the table puts a whole new slant on things – literally.

- **It can resaw thick timber**
Bandsaws with a powerful
motor of at least 1hp
(horsepower) have the
added advantage of being
able to resaw thick timber
into thinner pieces. This
means that square stock
can be easily resized into
flat stock, sawn veneers can
be created, and immensely
strong built-up laminations
– as often found in
contemporary furniture
design – can be made.

**RIGHT A thick piece of
Honduran mahogany
is being cut quickly and
accurately into narrow strips.**

1:2 Bandsaw anatomy

Any brand new bandsaw may look perfectly good with its casing shut. It is when you open the doors and explore its construction that you realize that not all bandsaws are made equal, especially if you have the opportunity to compare several different models. It pays to look beneath the surface when choosing a new machine. The better the design, the better the facilities it offers, the better the results you will get from it, and the longer it will last. A professional machine will cost more than an entry-level model, but you pay the price for a reason, and it will certainly repay the extra investment.

Professionals make much more intensive demands on their machinery, both in terms of work output and the capacity of the machine to handle large sections of timber, and in that context a bandsaw is likely to be used by several different craftsmen in the same workshop. The resultant heavier usage is obviously more punishing on the machines than those used by the home woodworker. In the garage or shed environment, however, a lightweight bandsaw is perfectly adequate, especially as it will invariably be better looked after, and carefully set up for use.

Anatomy of a medium-duty bandsaw (1)

These are the external features of a typical floor-standing saw. Other models will differ in detail, but the features shown are common to most bandsaws.

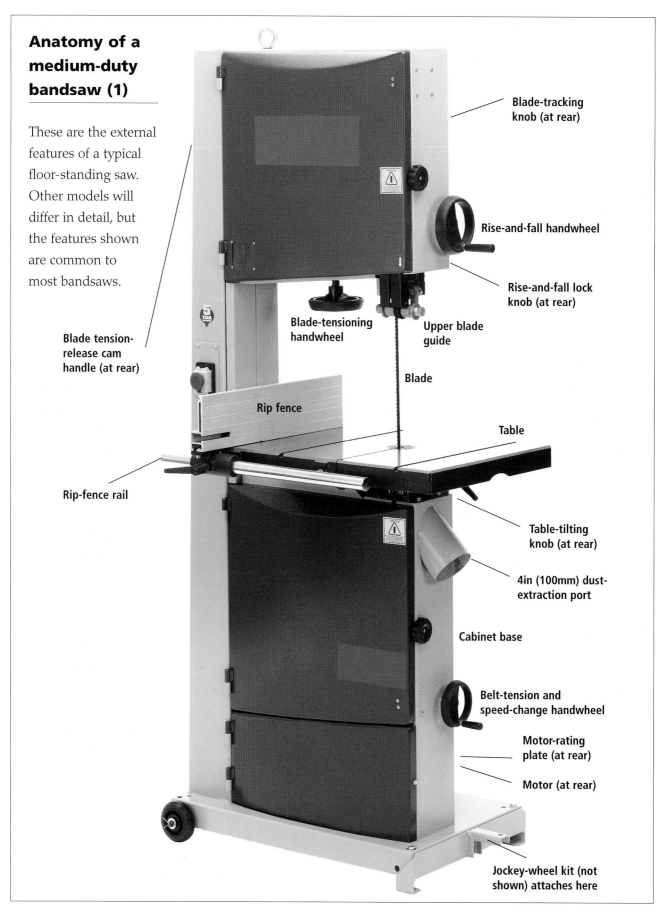

Blade-tracking knob (at rear)

Rise-and-fall handwheel

Rise-and-fall lock knob (at rear)

Blade tension-release cam handle (at rear)

Blade-tensioning handwheel

Upper blade guide

Blade

Rip fence

Table

Rip-fence rail

Table-tilting knob (at rear)

4in (100mm) dust-extraction port

Cabinet base

Belt-tension and speed-change handwheel

Motor-rating plate (at rear)

Motor (at rear)

Jockey-wheel kit (not shown) attaches here

Blade tension-release cam handle

The cam release, fitted to some newer machines, allows for quick detensioning when blade changing or stopping work at the end of the day.

Blade-tensioning handwheel

This is usually found on top of the upper case, or directly underneath or above the table.

Blade-tracking knob

This controls the degree of tilt on the upper bandwheel, which in turn determines the tracking position of the blade on the wheels. It should only be used when an adjustment is needed, otherwise it is left at the last effective setting.

Rise-and-fall handwheel

Used to adjust the guard covering the blade. It makes sense to keep the guard down as much as possible, to expose less blade and reduce flexing. A knob is provided to lock it in the correct position.

Upper blade guide

The upper blade-guide assembly not only supports the blade, but also keeps it running true. It is matched by a similar – although sometimes simplified – arrangement under the table.

Blade

Wide blades are easier to use; narrow blades need more care in setting up.

Rip fence

The rip fence allows you to cut parallel to the blade fairly accurately. Rip fences are often aluminium extrusions, although they can also be fabricated from folded pressed steel, or even cast metal.

Table

Tables are generally cast iron or occasionally cast aluminium. It is important to check the table flatness on any new acquisition before using it for work.

Table-tilting knob

The geared trunnions under the table are moved by a geared tilt knob. A lock knob prevents the table from sinking back to a level position.

4in (100mm) dust-extraction port

A large dust port is preferable; having two is even better, with extraction being made in two different places for maximum efficiency.

Cabinet base

Ideally this should be a rigid, pressed-steel, welded cabinet. The smooth running efficiency of a bandsaw depends on this rigidity.

Belt-tension and speed-change handwheel

It is necessary, when cutting metal in particular, to be able to change to a lower speed, although this won't be a frequent requirement. The handle allows tension to be slackened off, so the drive belt can be moved to the adjacent pulley wheels to effect the speed change.

Motor-rating plate

This indicates the machine's power requirements and speed in rpm (revs per minute). It should also give the country of origin and the manufacturer.

Motor

Motors for large machines are different from those for hand-held power tools. They are normally what are called induction motors, or they may have a 'capacitor start'. The motor should run more smoothly and quietly than a power tool.

Jockey-wheel kit

This optional accessory allows the bandsaw to be manoeuvred around easily, which can be useful in a small workshop.

Rip-fence rail

The fence slides along a rail which may have a scale to help with setting the cut width.

Anatomy of a bandsaw (2)

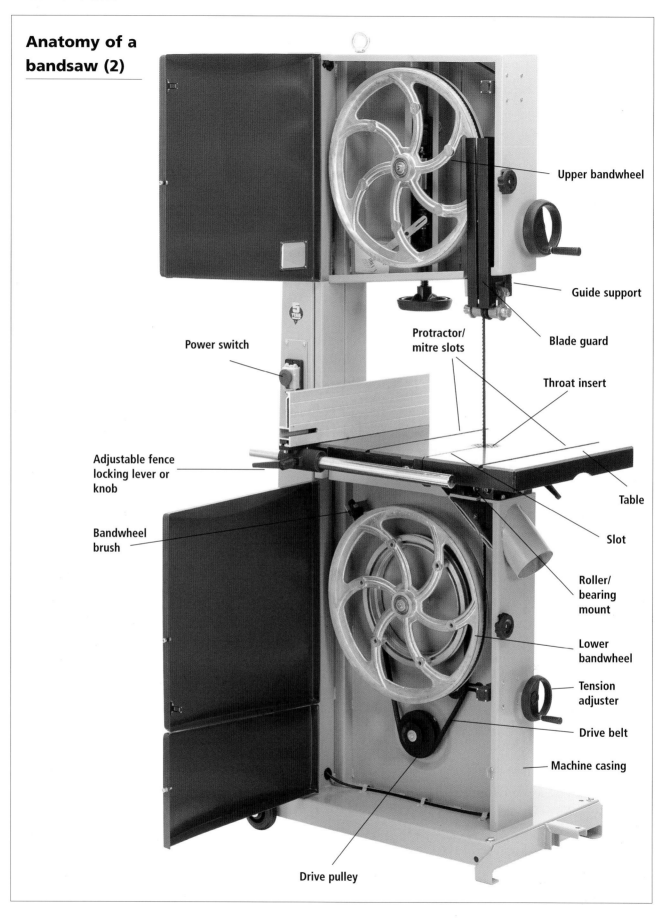

Upper bandwheel

Guide support

Power switch

Protractor/ mitre slots

Blade guard

Throat insert

Adjustable fence locking lever or knob

Table

Bandwheel brush

Slot

Roller/ bearing mount

Lower bandwheel

Tension adjuster

Drive belt

Machine casing

Drive pulley

Upper and lower bandwheels

The loop of the bandsaw blade is mounted on these wheels. They have either rubber or cork tyres to help the blade run smoothly.

Guide support

This holds the guide in place and allows it to move up and down. It can be positioned to allow the minimum area of blade to be exposed for safe cutting. A gap of ½in (12mm) above the work is about right.

Protractor/mitre slots

These machined grooves on the table run parallel to the blade, so a mitre gauge (protractor) can be used to regulate the angle of cut, allowing cuts from 90° to 45° to be made in either direction.

Blade guard

This protects the user from the exposed area of the blade as it exits the cover of the machine. It is adjusted up and down by a knob or lever alongside.

Throat insert

This small wooden or plastic section through which the blade passes is removable to allow replacement of the blade. It can be replaced when it is worn, or a custom-made insert can be fitted.

Table

This is the operating surface of the machine, which the blade runs through. On some machines it can be tilted and locked at different angles. The best tables are cast iron, or even cast aluminium.

Slot

This slot, machined all the way through the table, is designed to allow the blade to be removed and replaced when it is necessary. Often there will be a bolt at the front edge of the slot to hold the table halves dead level; this bolt is removed to facilitate blade replacement.

Roller/bearing mount

This part of the lower guide assembly contains the roller bearings, which support the blade, preventing excessive play and wear. Always choose a machine with good guide and roller support above and below the table.

Tension adjuster

This is used to adjust the tension of the blade. This will vary, depending on the size and type of blade.

Drive belt

This transmits the drive between the motor and the lower bandwheel.

Machine casing

This covers all the moving parts of the machine.

Drive pulley

This is either a single or double pulley fitted on the motor shaft. The double-sized allows two speeds.

Bandwheel brush

This removes sawdust from the lower bandwheel. It will require periodic adjustment.

Adjustable fence locking lever or knob

Once tightened, this prevents the fence from being moved. Fences that run the full length of the table will usually lock at the far end when you tighten the lever at the front. This prevents any chance of misalignment or movement during use.

Power switch

Normally the bandsaw is wired to the mains supply through a starter switch mounted on the casing. Usually a green button is on and a red off. This should be a no-volt-release switch, so that, if the power supply is interrupted – irrespective of whether the switch was previously on or off – it will not restart when the power supply is reconnected. This is an important safety feature.

Choosing a bandsaw

As with any other piece of new or secondhand machinery, there are many key features you need to examine in order to become conversant with the capabilities of the machine.

Price
Usually, the more money you pay the more power you get, but be aware that some important elements may feature on other less expensive machines.

Wheel diameter
There is a variety of sizes to choose from, most commonly from 14 to 18in (356–457mm). Blades as wide as ⅝in (16mm) are fine on a 14in (356mm) wheel. Resawing blades, which are wider and last longer, have far more traction on larger wheels. Some cheap models are very lightly built and may even be made from a heavy-grade plastic material. Cast bandwheels, whether alloy or cast iron, are much to be preferred. You may find a series of drillings at certain places around the wheel. This is part of the balancing process, to ensure the wheel runs smoothly at operating speed. The running surface of the wheel should have a slight camber or curve, and a rubber tyre or a layer of cork – to allow smooth running without blade damage.

Guides
Upper and lower guides hold the blade straight and stable. There are many guides to choose from, made from several types of material. Which ones you choose will be dependent on factors like cost, availability and which blade size is used most.

Aside from the rigidity of the casing and the running accuracy of the bandwheels, good guides are the third most important requirement in a good-quality machine. In some cases it is possible to retrofit superior third-party guide systems to improve cut reliability and reduce guide wear.

Tension-release lever
Try to remember to release tension on the blade at the end of a day's work, as this will help to maintain the blade for a longer period of time. In machines that do not have a lever, detensioning must be achieved using the tension-setting knob, which is slower.

Cutting height
The amount of clearance under the guides gives you the depth of cut allowable.

For the US market, the addition of a riser block (see pages 14 and 15) will allow the distance to be increased, enabling larger workpieces to pass through the blade. This is not available in the UK at the time of writing.

CAUTION

In a communal workshop detensioning overnight is not a good idea, as other users may not check the tension setting before starting work the next day.

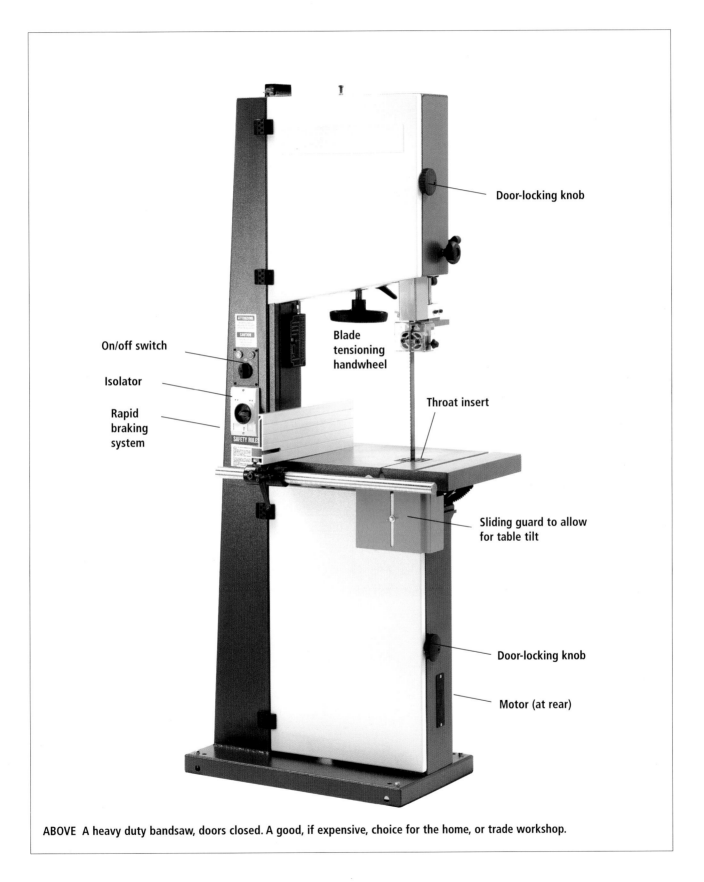

Door-locking knob

On/off switch

Isolator

Rapid braking system

Blade tensioning handwheel

Throat insert

Sliding guard to allow for table tilt

Door-locking knob

Motor (at rear)

ABOVE A heavy duty bandsaw, doors closed. A good, if expensive, choice for the home, or trade workshop.

Throat width

The wider the throat, the greater the board width that can be fed through the machine. Bigger bandwheels equal greater throat width, apart from on a few three-wheel machines, where extra wheel offset to the rear also gives greater throat capacity. Apart from the extra price you pay, there is the size and weight to consider when trying to fit a big machine into a compact workshop. However, for many purposes, an industrial model bandsaw may be a better choice than a cheap bandsaw and a cheap tablesaw, as it will outperform both quite easily.

Table

A cast-iron table will give greater stability, especially useful if you intend to resaw heavy logs. Pressed-steel tables are not only rather 'tinny' and noisy, but cannot give a guaranteed flat surface. However, even castings change shape slightly after machining, so you need to check that your table is truly flat using a straightedge. A good heavy table is a plus feature and, since it is where all workpieces have to lie, it is a vital component.

Adjustable fence

This can usually be positioned to either the left or right of the blade, depending on your personal preference and what type of cut you want to make.

The adjustable fence is used to help you guide the workpiece through the blade reasonably accurately. Once it is in position, you lock it by tightening a lock-nut (knob or lever). Some fence types can only be used to the left (casing) side of the blade. This is not so good if you want to do bevel cuts, for example, where ideally the workpiece should lie on the fence, using gravity to guide it safely through the blade.

Casing

A good case can be solid, stable and free of vibration, depending on the type of model chosen. Cheaper machines have a simple pressed-steel case; the more expensive machines have extra reinforcement to give more rigidity between the upper and lower parts of the case, thus reducing vibration and allowing more accurate cutting.

Power

Look for a machine over 1hp if possible, though 2hp is better for resawing. Big workshops usually have a three-phase supply installed, and you can take advantage of the larger motors this allows in big machines. However, for most users, single-phase is perfectly adequate, as these bandsaws do not demand as much power as some other machines used for woodworking.

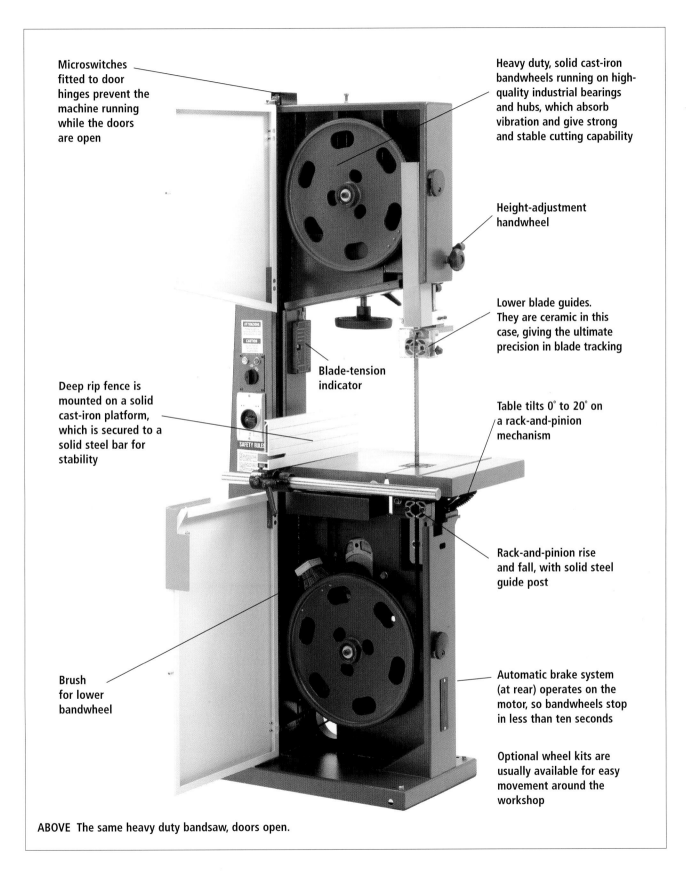

Microswitches fitted to door hinges prevent the machine running while the doors are open

Heavy duty, solid cast-iron bandwheels running on high-quality industrial bearings and hubs, which absorb vibration and give strong and stable cutting capability

Height-adjustment handwheel

Lower blade guides. They are ceramic in this case, giving the ultimate precision in blade tracking

Blade-tension indicator

Deep rip fence is mounted on a solid cast-iron platform, which is secured to a solid steel bar for stability

Table tilts 0° to 20° on a rack-and-pinion mechanism

Rack-and-pinion rise and fall, with solid steel guide post

Brush for lower bandwheel

Automatic brake system (at rear) operates on the motor, so bandwheels stop in less than ten seconds

Optional wheel kits are usually available for easy movement around the workshop

ABOVE The same heavy duty bandsaw, doors open.

Key components

Guide assemblies

These are provided both above and immediately below the table on most machines, with the top guide unit adjustable vertically to expose more or less of the bandsaw blade.

Guide assemblies provide accuracy and stability for the blade as it passes through the workpiece, both above and below the table. The guides therefore support the blade, and also limit both lateral and backward movement to the left and right using the side guides, and from behind using the thrust bearing or thrust wheel. The guide assemblies on lightweight machines are adequate, but those on better quality machines will give more accurate support.

There are metal, plastic, fibre, hardwood and ceramic side guides on the market. Whichever ones you choose, check periodically that they are not worn and correct those that are, as worn guides will never perform properly. There should be no contact between the guides and the teeth of the saw blade, so make sure both are properly positioned. Finally, set the thrust wheel, to prevent the blade being pushed backwards during a cut.

On the top guide unit, check that neither the saw guides nor the thrust wheel deflect the blade when moved between the extreme top and bottom positions. If this does happen, there may be some blade misalignment, so readjust if necessary, before attempting to reset the guides and thrust bearing.

The blade guides are located both above and below the table and both should be set correctly to achieve accurate cutting. If you are using smaller blades this is even more critical.

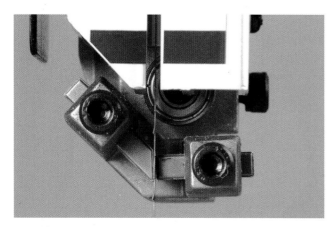

ABOVE Metal blade support blocks. Note how the left-hand block is angled, thus avoiding a conflict with the table when tilted. Located behind is the thrust bearing, which supports the back edge of the blade.

ABOVE In this model discs are used instead of blocks to support the blade. They are positioned just a short way back from the teeth, without actually touching them.

> **(◉ KEY POINT**
>
> Never set the thrust wheel hard against the blade, as this will damage both the blade and the thrust wheel itself. This fault gives itself away by a distinctive metallic scraping noise. If you hear this, stop the machine and investigate at once.

ABOVE **This is the manufacturer's own throat insert. It lies neatly, a fraction below the table surface, is relieved on the underside to allow it to tilt, and has holes for dust to drop through.**

Finally, refit the throat insert, but make sure that there is slot clearance behind the blade and that the insert does not bind on the blade below table level – either when the table is horizontal or when tilted to the full extent to right or left. To allow for this, the insert should be relieved on the underside only, to leave the smallest practical gap on either side of the saw at table level, regardless of the table setting.

Before running the saw, check that the bottom wheel brush, if fitted, is set correctly to prevent sawdust build-up, and connect the sawdust exit to a dust-extraction system. Make sure that this operates efficiently when the saw is in use, and close the exhaust-connection gate or slider when not using it, so that extraction effort is diverted to other connected machines. Make sure that all guards are fitted and properly set before using the machine. Always set the top guide to just clear the workpiece top – it must be set as described on page 56. Set your work lights, to illuminate the whole working area.

Ideally, blades should be changed when cutting wood of different thicknesses, or even curves of different radii. This is unlikely to happen in reality, as it means

changing the guide settings as well, and I suspect that many woodworkers leave a single blade *in situ* to tackle most of their sawing operations. However, if you are disciplined enough to switch blades for different tasks, then the guide system you choose should be one which is easily adjustable. If you are happy to work with a single blade, then any guide system will work for you, although of course some are better than others.

ABOVE **These hardened guide discs are set close but not tight on the blade. The 'thrust disc' behind is often not a disc but a bearing, although the effect is the same. It will tend to rotate when the blade touches against it.**

ABOVE **A typical under-table guide set-up.**

ⓚKEY POINT

The combination of the guides themselves and the adjustment mechanism which holds them is the key to a good-quality and effective system.

Blade guides

There are three different types of guide systems: ball-bearing, block and disc. The work you carry out and the range and size of blades you use should determine which system is right for you. Ideally, the guide system should be simple to set up, be able to support the width of a substantial blade, and need very little maintenance.

Ball-bearing guides have a long life, are low-maintenance and easy to set on wide blades; they are slightly more difficult on narrow blades, as there is a risk of contact with the teeth. The bearings come in different sizes and stacked, larger bearings offer better quality than smaller ones. As these run on the curve of the rollers, there is much less surface area contacting the blade, so heat and friction are reduced. The noise level is also reduced.

Block guides are the most versatile of the three choices, offering good service to both narrow and wide blades. They are shown in the box opposite.

ABOVE A set of well-used roller guides, which are still giving good service.

> ## FOCUS ON:
>
> ### Block guides
>
> There are four types:
> Care must be taken when setting **steel blocks**, as there is a tendency to dull the blade's teeth should there be contact. On narrow blades – such as ¼in (6mm) – this can present a problem. Any long-term friction will result in wear and tear on the face of the blocks. They must then be replaced, or ground or filed flat again.
>
>
>
> ABOVE These are good standard running blocks. Many owners like to replace them with hardwood, which is easy to replace at little cost.

Polymer blocks will not dull a blade as they are a softer material, but they will wear out more quickly than steel blocks. However regaining a flat surface to work with is a simple enough affair.

Phenolic blocks – also known as 'Cool' blocks, which is a trade name – are easy to work with, easy to set up, will not dull the blade, are hard-wearing and simple to dress flat. They can be pressed right up to the blade to give maximum support and keep the blade true and straight without damage.

Ceramic blocks are relatively new to the market and great claims are made for them. They are used primarily because of their heat-displacement properties, which enables them to run tight against the blade without heat build-up. However, ceramic blocks will still dull a blade's teeth should the two come into contact, as may happen with narrow blades, so setting up has to be precise and is a touch more time-consuming.

ABOVE **Polymer (plastic) guide blocks.**

ABOVE **Phenolic resin 'Cool' blocks. A popular material for critical applications, such as templates and jigs, as well as bandsaw guides.**

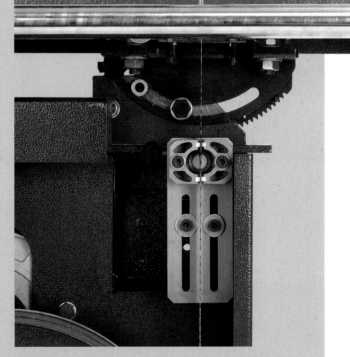

ABOVE **Ceramic guides are more expensive and only fit larger machines, but they give impressive accuracy.**

Disc guides (also known as European roller guides) offer a great deal of support to the blade. They have hardened faces, so there should be little or no wear and tear, but they must not touch the teeth of the blade.

On the downside, they can be difficult to set, and again the problem is with narrow blades. There can also be problems with minor wear on the inside of their shafts, which in turn can cause the discs to wobble and, in some circumstances, freeze. Should they need replacing, the whole unit must be changed, which can be expensive.

On better bandsaws, the guides and the thrust bearing – which sits directly behind the blade, preventing it from moving backwards – can be adjusted independently of each other: the thrust bearing can be moved before or after the guides have been set, which is perhaps the most effective system.

LEFT Because these discs are larger than standard blocks, they do need careful setting to avoid tooth contact.

Without this independence, the movement of the side guides automatically moves the thrust bearing, which can be slightly frustrating.

Some bandsaws may feature micro-adjusting nuts or cams, which should be easily accessible for precision placing of guides and thrust bearings. Without them, it is a case of either pushing or pulling the guides and bearings into place manually.

⒦KEY POINT

If you will be cutting thick timber and/or using hardwoods, then your machine will need a fair amount of horsepower behind it, in fact the more the better. More power means more speed and better quality, and your workpiece can be fed through the blade without slowing down the motor. When a motor does become bogged down, the blade will wander and give an irregular cut. As a general rule, for sawing hardwoods which are less than 2in (50mm) thick, then ¾hp should be plenty. With a motor of this size, resawing is achievable with most timber stock, providing the feed is monitored to ensure that the blade maintains its full speed at all times. A motor of 1hp would be preferable should the stock for resaw be up to 6in (152mm) thick, and timber of up to 12in (300mm) thick would really demand 1½ to 2hp.

LEFT All machines have a specification plate somewhere on the casing. It will express the motor power in either horsepower or kilowatts, or both.

(FOCUS ON:

Guide adjustments when changing blades

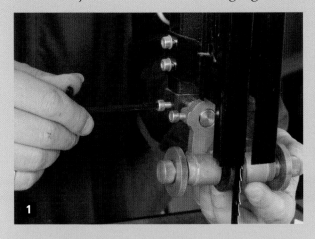

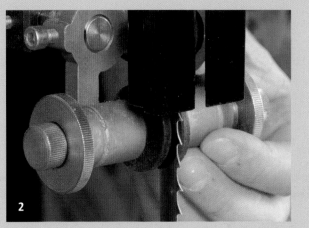

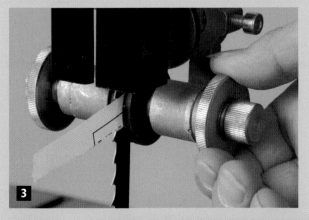

1 Open the side guides and move the thrust wheel to the rear before removing the blade.

2 Move the guide blocks out to the sides.

3 When the new blade is in place and has settled down in its running position, move the guide blocks so they just clear the tooth gullets, setting them against the blade without deflecting it.

4 Finally, set the thrust wheel so that there is a minimal gap between it and the back of the blade. A distance of around 1/32in to 1/16in (0.5mm to 1mm) is acceptable – a larger gap is not.

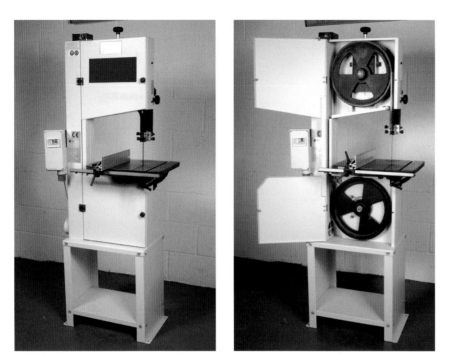

ABOVE This bandsaw gets around the problem of column strength by enclosing the entire column, just a narrow gap for blade access. A closed base would have made it even more stable.

ABOVE Bandsaws with a separate base can sometimes be less stable than an all-in-one design.

ABOVE The greater the reinforcement in the cabinet and column, the greater the overall stability of a closed-stand machine.

Frames and cabinets

Stability is a major consideration, and any operation which involves work of a larger scale, substantial pieces of timber, needs a stable machine. But because, like the lathe, the bandsaw is a very hands-on machine, which requires focus and a deft touch, you certainly get a feel for the working process. You will feel any vibration and come to know when the machine is running well. The larger, better-quality bandsaws have a welded-steel column which runs continuously from top to bottom of their cases. This makes them exceptionally sturdy and able to take a great deal of tension.

KEY POINT

There tends to be great variation in factors such as noise, vibration or degrees of upper-wheel flexibility under load. The design of the case – or more precisely the case reinforcement – will affect these factors. One model of smaller machine, for instance, has a bent pipe welded to the rear of the case. This makes for an incredible degree of rigidity on what is otherwise not a particularly big machine. Always look for evidence of this kind of extra design endeavour intended to improve case rigidity.

Resaw capacity

A bandsaw with a 12in (300mm) throat should suffice for the majority of resawing tasks. Should you possess a model with less capacity, say 6–8in (152–200mm) throat clearance, this may well be ample for some, if not all, of your bandsaw needs. However, the rule, as with most other workshop machinery, is 'the bigger the better' – bigger meaning more power as well as greater capacity.

Wheel diameter

The principal advantage of larger-diameter wheels is that they are able to hold saw blades of a greater width, which are substantially better for ripping and resawing. Greater traction and transmission of power is possible because the blade contacts a greater surface area than on smaller-diameter wheels. Resawing is covered in greater depth in 'Basic Bandsawing Principles' (pages 112–14).

Thicker blades also have more longevity on larger wheels: blades up to ½in (12mm) wide, are usually 0.025in (0.6mm) thick, and most ¾in (19mm) blades are thicker at 0.032in (0.8mm) or more. In general, carbide-tipped blades are thicker still. The greater the diameter of the wheel, the less prone thick blades are to premature breakage from metal fatigue, because they will bend to a lesser degree than if rotating over a tighter radius.

The diameter of most bandsaws wheels is roughly 14in (356mm), but the significant advantages of even bigger wheels are:

- Larger throat capacity – every extra inch in wheel diameter means an extra inch to work with between the support column and the blade.
- Larger blades can handle thicker and harder workpieces more easily, though wide blades break relatively easily and prematurely.

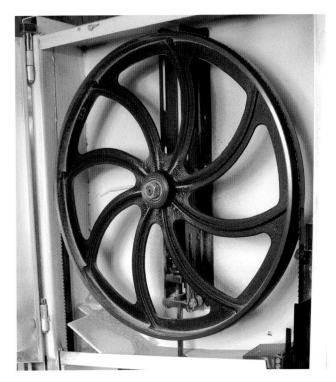

ABOVE A large and rather unusual design of bandwheel.

LEFT Blades come in many combinations of width and tooth configuration.

ⓘKEY POINT

Many bandsaws claim to be able to take a ¾in (19mm) blade (an adequate width for most jobs in the workshop), but running a blade of this size on a 14in (356mm) machine is not always practical, as the blades are too thick. Although this size of blade is less prone to bending in the cut than a narrower blade, with care you can still achieve good results with ½in (12mm) or smaller blades, and even with very thin blades, down to ⅛in (3mm). Although all machines can handle a blade of this size, they are better suited to some machines, mainly due to the fact that some guides are more easily set than others.

Table size and rigidity

At some point you will probably have to work with larger lengths of timber and wider stock. If your bandsaw has a big enough table to support the work, that's great. But unless you go for a more heavy-duty and hence more expensive model, it is likely that you will struggle to support larger workpieces. Extension tables may be available or, with a little ingenuity and time, you can design and fit your own. But a strong, stable and rigid table will improve a saw's performance. Unfortunately the tables on many domestic bandsaws are just too small and too unstable for many woodworking tasks other than small-scale work.

LEFT A small bench-top machine cannot cope with larger sections but is capable of quite good smaller work so long as it is not pushed beyond its intended limits.

ABOVE This table has a small extension to allow the fence to run off the main table, which provides a larger usable work area.

Tension-release knob, wheel or lever

To achieve accurate results on a bandsaw it is essential that the blade is tensioned correctly and, because there are huge stresses generated when a blade is tensioned, it is vitally important that this component is designed for maximum strength and rigidity.

A heavy-duty spring mechanism is the key to maintaining tension. Some bandsaws have useful indicators showing the degree of tension in the blade as the adjusting mechanism is tightened.

The introduction of quick-release tension levers certainly helps. Some loosen the blade enough to facilitate easy blade changing – a great time saver – while others merely adjust the tension, which helps prevent the tyres from suffering. The controls should be located for easy access above or below the upper cabinet.

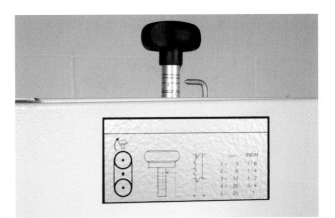

ABOVE A neat design with a pointer for tensioning against rings marked on the knob shaft and a handy chart for blade tension selection.

ⓀKEY POINT

Most woodworkers know that, at the end of a working day, you should detension the bandsaw blade by loosening the appropriate knob or lever – which is usually located on top of the machine – but how many, I wonder, actually carry out this operation? The reasons for doing so, however, are sound: it prevents flat spots on the rubberized tyres around the wheels, and also prolongs the life of the blade.

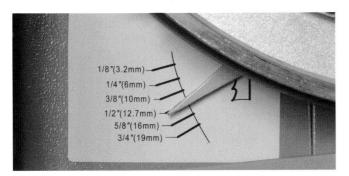

ABOVE A neat, accurate means of tensioning, but located inside the case and only accessible with the door open.

ABOVE A less helpful example of a tensioning indicator. Apart from the word 'max' there is no suggestion of what the correct tension might be.

Blade observation window

This is a feature that takes the inconvenience out of tracking a blade (see 'Tracking the blade' in 'Setting up and Maintenance', page 54) but it is not available on all machines.

The blade must sit correctly on the wheels and, to get a new blade centred, the angle of the upper wheel usually needs be tilted a few degrees either way. The standard method is to open the upper cabinet and slowly spin the wheel by hand, gauging the movement of the blade back and forth over the wheel surface or 'crown'. When the angle of the upper wheel is correct (adjusted by the blade-tracking wheel or knob) the blade will remain centred.

With an observation window, the bandsaw can be switched on, and you can then observe the blade in action and its position on the wheel. It can be finely adjusted, speeding up considerably what might otherwise be a rather laborious task. Set the basic positioning on the wheels first, before closing the case doors, otherwise the blade may come off the wheel.

Dust ports

Dust collection is often inadequate on bandsaws. Those with smaller ports – especially the 2½in (63mm) type – have little impact, and larger ports, 4in (100mm) for example, fare much better. Having two ports is better still: the upper one, located below the table, will extract dust directly from the blade, whilst the lower port carries away wood debris from the bottom of the wheel cavity. The real problem is that the design of bandsaw cases allows dust to settle in a compacted lump in the bottom. The better the extraction, the less likely this is to happen. A downwards-angled port, located just under the table and around the guide assembly, is favoured because it catches most of the dust as it is freshly generated.

ABOVE A window allows you to view the blade tracking position safely while the machine is running.

ABOVE A port at the bottom of the casing is more usual but not particularly helpful, as the dust will already have collected around the bottom bandwheel.

Dust ports usually incorporate some means of preventing finger entry, to prevent accidents when trying to clear dust manually while the machine is still plugged in.

Because bandsaw dust tends to compact very easily, a powerful extractor is important, even though the bandsaw does not appear to be a machine that needs it, especially when compared to the prodigious output of a planer-thicknesser, or even a tablesaw.

Inefficiently extracted bandsaws tend to suffer from excess sawdust literally stuck on both bandwheels, particularly the lower one, and this dust – which can affect the smooth running of the blade – is very difficult to remove by scraping, without damaging the running surface of the bandwheel. For this reason it is important to prevent dust building up in the first place. In the example below, the internal chute is rectangular, but changes to a standard round bore external pipe fitting. (See also 'Dust extraction', page 97.)

ABOVE An intelligently designed dust-removal system with a chute directly below the blade area and thence to the downward-angled port.

ABOVE Another form of direct dust exit from the blade area; the baffle across part of the port is presumably intended to increase the suction effect.

Rip fence

The sturdier this is, the better, particularly for short joinery cuts. But, having said that, a major consideration when using the fence – especially for ripping or resawing – is that the operation often requires a slight adjustment to the angle of the fence when cutting long, straight lines. The reason for this is to compensate for blade drift (known as 'lead'), which will occur less with larger machines with wider, stronger blades, but on more domestic machines is an all too common occurrence.

If you can find a fence with easy angle adjustment this is worth considering, though few seem to provide this facility.

ABOVE A standard non-tilting fence. This one runs on two rails at back and front of the table, allowing it move right off the table to the left for greater capacity. Note the unusual removable 'point fence' attachment halfway along.

ABOVE Fences are frequently made from aluminium extrusions. This one can be swapped around so that a very low edge is available for cutting thin material. It has a middle clamping position but no support at the end furthest from the operator.

Tilting table

Most bandsaws possess this feature, usually tilting to the right. However, the removal of the 90° stop (underneath the table on the tilting protractor head) may allow for a degree of left tilt. This facility is useful for cutting angled tenons as well as dovetail joints.

ABOVE The principle of the geared, locking trunnion system for tilting tables is clearly shown here. At the far right is an adjustable bolt resting on the casing to give the standard 90° position.

LEFT Extreme tilt on this bandsaw gives a position well past the standard 45° found on most machines.

BELOW The trunnion mechanism is clearly revealed on this machine. The tilt knob and locking lever are at the rear. Note the thrust bearing, which is unusually edge-on to the blade and mounted on a square post.

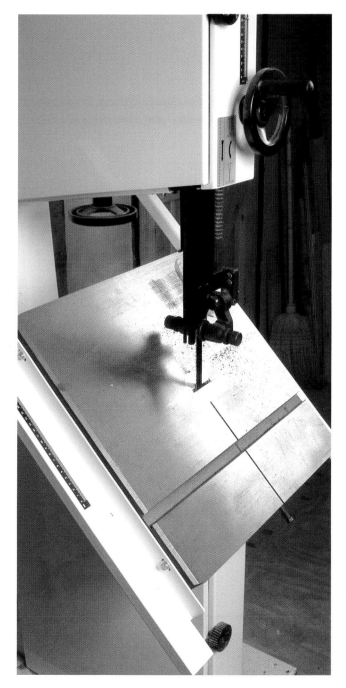

ABOVE **The pulley belt is discreetly hidden behind the lower bandwheel. In this case the knob and lock lever (lower left) are used to slacken off and then retighten the belt when doing a speed change. This makes it much easier to move the belt across.**

KEY POINT

Be extremely careful if you change from wood cutting to metal cutting. Wood dust is highly inflammable and all dust must be thoroughly cleaned away first, as any stray sparks from the workpiece or blade could be very dangerous.

Changing speed

Altering the speed of a bandsaw can be a useful resource to have, although it is not always an option. It is unusual for a bandsaw to have a step-pulley system, whereby the transmission belt from the motor is adjustable between larger or smaller pulley wheels linked to the lower wheel of the bandsaw.

By this system the speed of the blade can be changed, allowing more effective cutting of different materials. For example, if cutting metal, a much slower speed is needed than for cutting wood – allied to the correct blade for the job, of course.

ABOVE **This machine is unusual as it is a single-speed-only model intended for wood, not for metal cutting. The vertical belt arrangement allows the weight of the motor to help tension the belt.**

Although is difficult to find all the good points in one machine, it is possible, by doing your research, to find a satisfactory compromise. This book is a good starting point in that search.

Nowadays, it is perfectly possible to browse, order and buy machinery online, but there is a dearth of good, visitable machinery dealers on the high street. The marketplace is quite cut-throat and most bandsaws are made in Italy and the Far East, these being where the mass-manufacturing expertise lies. However, it is a good idea to locate those tool dealers that do exist within reasonable striking distance and pay them a visit. Apart from being able to have a 'hands-on' experience, it is possible to discuss pros and cons with the dealers, who should have good knowledge of the ranges they sell.

There is another opportunity when dealers have their demonstration days. These are generally friendly, convivial affairs with a trained demonstrator showing the full range of tasks that a machine can perform – plus the company of like-minded woodworkers and refreshments, of course! If you happen to know any professional or amateur woodworkers, why not take advantage of their experience relating to bandsaws?

If you finally decide to buy by mail order or online, you need to bear in mind the following points: although it is a legitimate way of making a transaction, you will – or should – be covered if a machine is faulty, and the supplier should replace your machine without charge. However, if it is simply a case of not performing as you had hoped, the supplier could well argue that it is performing as intended within its price and specification. The onus is therefore on you, the purchaser, to ensure that you choose a machine fit for your purposes. If it isn't, then you could be stuck with an expensive and unwanted acquisition.

ABOVE A brand-new bandsaw is put through its paces. It is sensible to wear ear defenders, but better to avoid long sleeves when using machinery.

1:3 Setting up and maintenance

As with any other machinery used for woodcutting, to ensure smooth running and safe operation, bandsaws require careful setting up before satisfactory work can be undertaken. Taking this process seriously is crucial and educational because it will help to familiarize you with the workings of the bandsaw and its functions, so it is well worth the initial effort.

The information in this chapter should be read in conjunction with the owner's manual, which will alert you to any peculiarities of your particular model. If you did not get a manual with the bandsaw, it should be available from the manufacturers, or you might even be able to download it from their website.

Internal mechanisms

Motor

One of the major sources of discontent with many bandsaws is the level of vibration when in operation, but a good motor should contribute to the smooth running of a machine and not add to problems of vibration (see 'Pulley wheels', right). There should be little or no play in the belt, and the motor should be properly fixed and stable in its housings.

By removing the drive belt and pulley you can observe the motor running freely, and check that its mountings are correctly set. If not, tighten up any loose fixings and, if there are still problems, you may be able to exchange the motor under warranty, or in the last resort buy a new one if it is out of warranty. However, in general motors are well built and operate smoothly, and are usually only sourced from manufacturers who specialize in motors and associated equipment.

Pulley wheels

These hold the drive belt(s) running from the motor to the drive wheel. For smooth running the two wheels should be correctly aligned, and set securely on their respective drive shafts. These are perhaps the first things to check if there is excess vibration. Failing this, the problem may be with the pulley wheels themselves. Less expensive bandsaws in particular have die-cast pulleys, which may not be perfectly round and may even need replacing. It pays to buy a better-quality machine and so avoid basic problems like this right at the start.

ABOVE This modern motor is not only powerful but relatively quiet; most noise is actually generated by the drive train – the bandwheels and blade. The cylinder on the side is the capacitor which helps kick the motor into life, giving full drive power almost instantaneously.

ABOVE Access to the pulley wheels is usually difficult because it has to be from behind the lower bandwheel. In this case it is made easier because a geared rack-and-tooth system allows the motor to be slackened off while performing the changeover.

Drive belts

As with all belt-driven machinery, worn or slack belts on the pulley wheels will cause vibration, so, if necessary, move the motor into a better position to tension up the belt. There is normally a means of doing this – adjustment slots and bolts, for example. A slack belt will potentially also cause a lack of drive power. Normally this isn't an issue on a bandsaw, although a well-used secondhand machine may have belt trouble. Belts come in different types, from flat 'poly-vee', to a single belt, to a belt with what look like teeth on the underside, which simply help the belt grip around plain pulley wheels. The net result of all these methods is very similar drive characteristics, but they should always be replaced with the same pattern of belt.

Table

The table must be level and flat – check this with a spirit level and straightedge. Whether new or old, a table casting can be distorted. Anything more than a small surface discrepancy, such as a bow or a 'wind' (twist), constitutes a problem. On a new machine it is a warranty issue. If you have purchased a secondhand machine and it is not flat, you can have the table ground flat. However, this can be an expensive option and is a matter of last resort.

The table must be square to the blade for a straight and true rip or crosscut, so use an accurate engineer's or combination square to check this. If it isn't square, adjust the table using the trunnions located underneath which, when unlocked, can move the table to the required angle. Many bandsaws have a 90° locking position underneath the table to keep it perpendicular for accurate cutting. If there is a 90° stop it may need adjustment once the table is locked dead square.

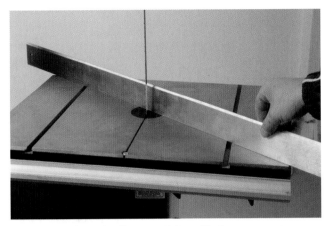

ABOVE Checking the flatness of the table from corner to corner as well as side to side can be instructive. An apparently flat-ground casting can turn out to be bowed when checked. The process of casting and machining can easily distort it out of the correct shape.

ABOVE Use the most accurate square you have to check whether the table is exactly perpendicular to the tensioned bandsaw blade. Many woodworkers favour an engineer's square rather than the common try square shown here, because they are made with greater precision.

There is often a bolt screwed into the end of the table slot which must be removed to change blades. When this bolt is replaced it assists the levelling of the table surface.

The table insert should have reasonable clearance around the blade and be flush with the table. A cheap and easy alternative is to replace the manufacturer's insert with a home-made one in ply or MDF, which will not damage the blade.

LEFT The table-levelling bolt must always be replaced after a belt change. Have a full set of workshop tools such as Allen keys and spanners (wrenches) handy at all times.

ABOVE If you want to make a ply or MDF insert, it will probably need a rebate on the underside to enable it to sit level in the hole. This can be done quite easily with a router and a bearing-guided cutter.

Guide post

The blade guard, the guide bearing and the thrust bearing are fitted to the guide post, which travels up and down to allow clearance for the thickness of the wood being cut. It may have a geared action via a knob on the case, or just a simple lift-and-lock action. The post must travel perpendicularly to the table, otherwise it may change the gap between the rear of the blade and the thrust bearing. If this happens, the guides and thrust bearing will need to be reset each time the post is moved up and down. To avoid this it may be necessary to retrack the bandsaw blade on the bandwheels so it is properly centred on both.

ABOVE The guide post has to incorporate several functions: holding the guides, moving up and down (often using gearing), and providing guarding. In this case there is a sliding guard plate that moves up and down with the post, to give continuous safe blade coverage.

Blades

The more commonly used blades range from $\frac{1}{4}$ to 1in (6–25mm) with 1.5 to 12tpi (teeth per inch). The larger blades with fewer tpi are used for large and deep cutting on dense woods, while smaller blades with more tpi are used for fine cutting and curved work (see Table on page 81). For more information on blades and setting them up, see Chapter 1.4, pages 73–89.

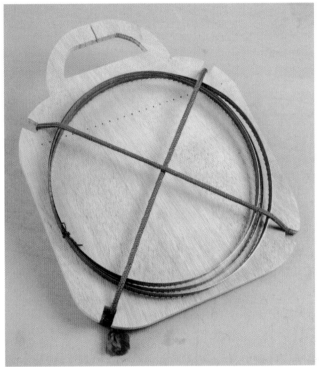

ABOVE A simple home-made blade carrier, using a bungee cord to secure the blade.

KEY POINT

Care should be taken at all times to avoid damaging the saw blade. When not in use, narrow bandsaw blades should be coiled into thirds (see page 84), secured and stored in a safe, dry place. Before use check for damaged teeth and cracks. Transport blades in a suitable home-made holder.

The blade guard is most important for safety and must not be removed. In many cases it is integral to the guide-post assembly, so it cannot be taken off.

ABOVE Only work on the back of the blade, and keep both file and fingers away from the teeth, which are very sharp.

For smooth and accurate running, check the joint where the blade is welded together: if it is thicker than the remainder, file or carefully grind it to the same thickness. To improve the running performance of the blade, use a fine file to lightly round off the back of the blade and remove any excess weld, taking great care while the machine is running. This will allow free blade movement and improved accuracy in the cut, whilst protecting the thrust wheel from excessive wear and tear.

Basic setting up

Tensioning

Tension is the minimum amount of stretch you must apply to the body of the bandsaw blade to make it stable. Tensioning is the most important single factor affecting the saw's performance.

ABOVE As the pressure is applied the tension knob can become quite stiff to turn. This is a good thing and means that you are coming up towards the correct tension setting.

Adjustments for tensioning and centring the saw blade are provided on all bandsaws, even though the method may vary slightly from one machine to another.

Assuming that a sharp blade has been fitted over the bandwheels in accordance with the manufacturer's instructions, with a little tension on the blade, rotate the upper wheel by hand in a clockwise direction with the power disconnected, at the same time increasing the tension on the blade by use of the adjustment knob on top of the machine.

Some bandsaws have tension scales, but these are not very accurate and can only be used as a guide for work up to 2½in (63mm) thick. When you are happy with the tension (see caption below), put a piece of masking tape alongside the tension scale at the rear of the top cover, then mark and record which size of blade it is for. The tension must be released after use at the end of a working session, otherwise the blade may eventually get fractionally stretched, causing the scale to be even more inaccurate.

It may take some trial and error before you arrive at the tension that suits you for each blade. However, a satisfactory check can be made by taking the blade between the forefinger and thumb, and applying slight finger pressure until a 2–3mm (1⁄16–1⁄8in) deflection of the blade is obtained. If your machine has a scale fitted to the tensioning device, follow the manufacturer's instructions. Of course, common sense has to be used – obviously, a 3⁄16in (5mm) blade requires less pressure to obtain the stated deflection than a 3⁄4in (19mm) blade.

RIGHT The deflection test is literally a 'rule of thumb'. If there is only a small deflection when pressed sideways, then the blade is at about the right tension.

ABOVE There has always been debate about the correct position of the blade on the bandwheels. This shows it too far forward in my opinion, although traditionalists using non-hardened blades like this position.

KEY POINT

Sometimes just running the blade in the direction of cut may cause it to jam, or come off the bandwheels, despite your best efforts. If you suspect that it is about to happen, you can undo the problem before it gets too serious: run the blade backwards for a few turns, tilt the upper wheel in the correct direction, then run the blade forward again. This time it should sit more happily in the middle of the bandwheel.

Tracking the blade

Continue rotating the upper wheel by hand, observing the position of the blade at the highest point of the wheel. It should lie on the curved surface of the tyre, approximately in its centre. Use the upper-wheel tilting device to adjust the position of the blade: turning one way will cause the blade to run to the front of the tyre, while turning it the other way will cause the blade to run towards the rear; the direction may vary from one machine to another. This procedure is known as tracking the blade. A degree of subtlety is needed for this operation. Any bandsaw user would have to admit to accidentally getting the tracking wrong, resulting in the blade coming off and catching inside the case. This is a bit scary when it happens, and the blade gets blunted in the process. Having the upper wheel reasonably upright first and making very slight tracking adjustments by turning the bandwheel by hand – power off, of course – is the best way, although some industrial models do not allow this, due to the built-in safety microswitching. When set to your satisfaction, set the locking knob to secure the blade in the correct location.

If the wheels of the saw are properly aligned, and the tyres are crowned (curved) adequately, the blade should track into position without your having to tilt the upper wheel away from its normal setting. However, some adjustment is almost inevitable.

ABOVE The blade is roughly centred on the camber of the wheel; this should ensure the blade is angled directly forward for correct cutting, helping to minimize 'lead'.

ABOVE Here the blade is clearly too far back on the wheel.

ABOVE Turning the upper bandwheel, while sighting the blade position and adjusting the tilt wheel with the other hand. Once it is correct it should be possible to spin the wheel by hand with the blade position remaining constant.

Guides

ABOVE A well set-up guide system with minimal gaps either side of the blade, the blade running comfortably in its true path.

Adjustable guides are provided to prevent the blade from twisting, to ensure the blade enters the work accurately, and to give support to the back of the blade when cutting. Failure to adjust guides to the correct tolerance can cause excessive wear of the blade, as well as difficulty in maintaining correct adjustment of the other guides, resulting in unsatisfactory cutting performance from what may be an otherwise excellent machine.

The upper guide assembly

Enclosing the bandsaw blade are the side guides which, to prevent any damage to the teeth themselves, must be adjusted to rest just a fraction behind the gullets between the teeth.

Adjust the side guide units – so they almost touch the bandsaw blade without deflecting or clamping it – by manipulating the adjusting screws or knobs as required. The guides must be kept separate from the blade while it is stationary, just by the thickness of a piece of paper – a distance that is close enough to support the blade should it begin to wander during a cut. To achieve this, place pieces of paper between each guide and the blade so that they are just gripped in place, lock the guides into position, then remove the pieces of paper. The guides should prevent the blade from twisting in use, but the blade must be allowed to run freely between them. Spinning the upper bandwheel by hand will show if the blade is free-running or not.

FOCUS ON

Home-made guide blocks

ABOVE Here oak blocks have been used for the side supports. Note the serious amount of wear on the rear thrust bearing caused by repeated lack of care in setting up – it urgently needs changing.

Replacing the metal block guides on your bandsaw with hand-cut wooden ones can produce good results. Try a tough hardwood such as jarrah, which should result in an improved performance with straight line and curved cutting, in retention of blade sharpness and reduction of breakage. However, wear on the wooden guides is fairly rapid, particularly when using a narrow blade, because the set of the teeth tends to wear the front edges of the guides and accuracy of cutting will be lost.

A better solution still is to use small blocks of Corian offcut. As Corian is tough and effectively self-lubricating, it improves guide life.

ABOVE A pair of guide blocks cut from a Corian offcut and sanded to size.

Thrust bearings or wheels

To complete the blade support, set the upper and lower thrust wheels to the back edge of the blade, leaving a gap of $\frac{1}{16}$in (2mm). The thrust wheels themselves should not spin until contact with the blade is made during cutting.

ABOVE The guides and thrust bearing can be moved independently for easier adjustment.

Bottom guides

Most saws have bottom guides using a similar set-up to the upper guides, with two side guides and a rear thrust wheel. Some are fixed to the main frame of the machine, but they can be adjusted in the same way as the top guides.

For correct running of the bandsaw you must adjust the bottom guides. Some guides are fitted on a shaft, which can be removed from the saw. Turning the guide over if possible (so the side guide rollers are at the top, closer to the top guide rollers) will reduce the distance between the rollers, so giving increased lateral support. Note: this will affect the ability of the table to tilt.

Use a piece of paper to adjust the side-roller clearance, so that the guide is set just behind the gullet of the blade and there is no more than $\frac{1}{16}$in (2mm) between the rear of the blade and the thrust bearing. This set-up takes a bit of time and patience but, when mastered, will give you the best results.

ABOVE Bottom guides set up with a 'paper gap' to both sides.

Fence

Most blades will 'lead' to one side when cutting, and most bandsaws do not cut square to the fence. Some fences can adjust sideways slightly to compensate for this tendency.

To determine the direction of cut for each blade, use a piece of ¼in (6mm) MDF slightly longer than the table length and about 6in (152mm) wide and, using a pencil marking gauge, mark a line parallel to the MDF edge. With the machine running, cut freehand down the line until about halfway. Stop the machine and carefully clamp the MDF back and front to the table.

Now butt the fence up to the edge of the test piece, adjust it to the angle of the test piece and lock it into place. It may be wise to use a sliding bevel square to record the angle on an offcut for future reference. Every time you change a blade, you *may* need to adjust the fence to suit. However, experience may show that one fence setting suits other blades quite satisfactorily. Obviously, if you tend to use just one or two blade types or sizes this extra adjustment is not such a big deal.

For added versatility it is simple enough to make your own fences to different heights and longer than the table length, using a sliding bevel square and a clamp to fix them to the table at the required width of cut.

If your fence isn't readily adjustable it may be possible to use a shim of some kind – perhaps even just paper, cardboard or sandpaper – placed behind the fence sub-face and fixed through the fence with screws.

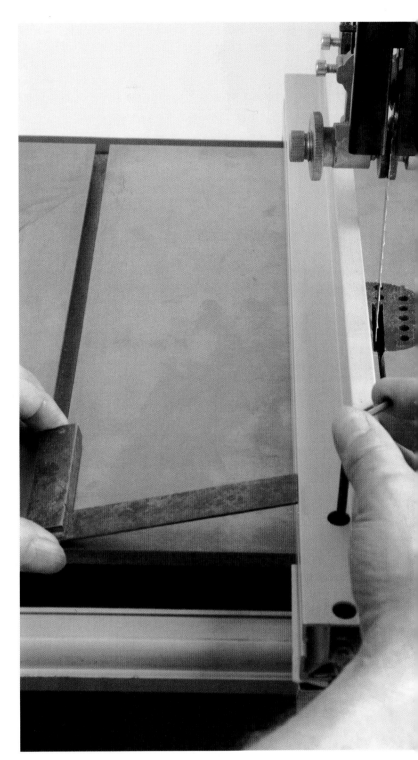

ABOVE Here is a technique for adjusting the fence to its 'default' position: lay a square in the mitre slot, adjusting the fence with its bolts loose until it just touches the square at both ends, then tighten the bolts. Further adjustment may be necessary to account for a 'lead' on the blade – remember this is the initial setting only.

Technique

Setting the fence angle

If there is a definite problem achieving a parallel fenced cut, try the following:

1 Mark a parallel line down a board and cut freehand exactly along the line.

2 Stop halfway through the cut and bring the fence up to the edge of board, which may result in a gap.

(If there is no gap, no further adjustment will be required and the fence is ready for use.)

3 Slacken off the fence adjusting bolts and set it until it neatly touches the board from end to end.

4 Your fence is now 'personalized' to your particular blade and tracking combination.

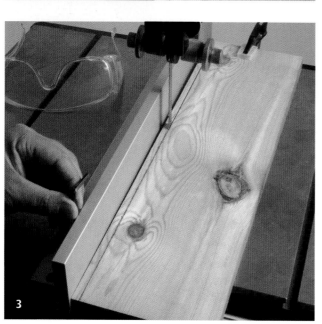

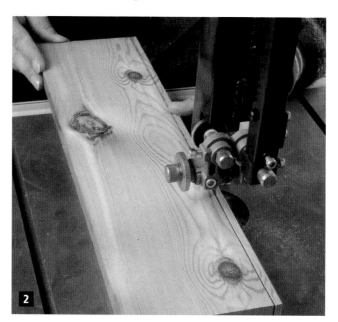

Testing the bandsaw set-up

When these procedures are completed, close the machine up and carry out the following tests:

1 Adjust the top guide assembly until it is approximately ½in (12mm) above the work to be cut. Draw a straight line on a piece of wood and make a test cut. Check that the cut is not only straight but also vertically square.

2 Mark a straight line on the wood and observe how readily the blade follows this line when pressed firmly against the fence. Following on from fence setting, the cut should be fine. However, if the saw tends to cut to one side, turn the wheel-tilt adjuster about half a turn in the direction that brings the cut straight (this depends on your particular model of bandsaw). Only a small amount of adjustment is required to bring about a considerable change.

The position of the blade-guide assembly will now require a minor adjustment to suit the altered position of the blade: if the saw cut is not already perpendicular, adjust the table so that it is at right angles to the blade. Should the saw cut be hollow in the middle, blade tension is insufficient, so increase tension.

When saw cuts tend to wander, check for wear of the side guides. Most guides can be removed and filed flat, so that maximum support is given to the blade.

If, after carrying out all of the above adjustments, difficulty is still encountered with straight cutting – particularly when using a rip fence – the blade itself must become suspect. Due to the method of manufacture or sharpening, some blades tend to lead in one direction.

To counteract the lead, clamp a waste block of wood to the saw table so that it touches the side of the blade opposite to the direction in which the saw tends to cut. Turn the bandwheel by hand only, while holding a slipstone against the teeth on the opposite side to the waste block, as the blade is rotated. Half a dozen turns should suffice. The purpose of this action is to remove the burr created when the blade has been sharpened from one side only.

ABOVE If the blade is cutting straight, then naturally the cut will be straight; it should also be perpendicular to the table.

ABOVE A marking gauge will give a very accurate line to cut to. This should show clearly whether the blade is on track. Any tendency to still cut off-line obviously needs adjustment.

SAFETY

NEVER place a file or slipstone against the blade teeth when the machine is running.

Wheel alignment

If you have followed the procedures above and the blade still tends to run off the wheel, change it and see if the problem occurs with one particular blade only. Not all bandsaw blades are perfect, and there are two problems sometimes found, particularly with new or resharpened wider blades:

1 The blade has not been joined squarely, resulting in the back of the blade being longer than the front (or vice versa).
2 If the teeth have been heat-treated in order to harden them, the front of the blade may contract on cooling, once again giving an uneven front-to-back length.

Both of these faults are difficult to correct. Fortunately this is not a common problem but, if it does occur, a great deal of time can be spent trying to figure out just what is going on. To be honest, if a blade is faulty the safest action is to discard it, as cutting and rebrazing are best left to a saw doctor who will charge more than the blade is worth.

(KEY POINT

When the saw is used frequently and/or by different operators, it is probably better to leave the machine set up ready to run. The only time the tension has been altered or adjusted on the writer's present bandsaw has been to change the blade. After ten years of fairly constant use, close inspection reveals no wear or serious deformation on the tyres or the tension spring. However, for the individual user more care will reap benefits, because your machine will be more finely tuned than a communal machine.

A more common cause of the problem is misaligned bandwheels. To align the wheels:

1 Install the widest blade that you usually use.
2 Adjust tension as explained previously, open the side panels and tilt the table as far as it will go (you may need to unbolt the table in order to check properly).
3 Position a long straightedge so that it touches both wheels, as close to centre as the hubs will permit. If the straightedge touches the top and bottom of both wheels, the wheels are parallel and lie in the same plane.
4 Should the top wheel not be parallel with the lower wheel, use the wheel-tilting handwheel to correct it.

If the wheels are parallel but do not lie in the same plane, two choices are usually available:

1 Adjust the lower, driven wheel which is locked onto the drive shaft, to bring it in line with the upper wheel.
2 Pack out the upper wheel with a suitable-sized washer or metal shim to line up with the lower wheel. In either case both wheels must be parallel and in line for correct operation.

If the wheels are distorted there is very little the average user can do about it, except to see that the mounting of the drive shaft has not become loose. Following any adjustment to the wheels, both the upper and lower blade guides will need to be readjusted.

ABOVE Checking whether the bandwheels are in line using a reliable straightedge.

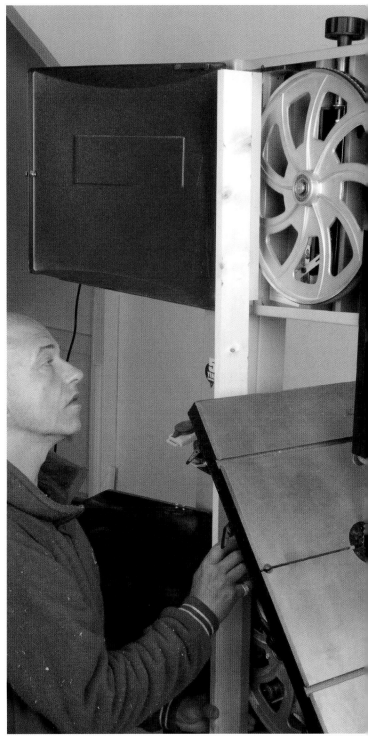

ABOVE Where it is not possible to hold a straightedge against both wheels because the casing interferes, make up a wooden straightedge with two glued and pinned strips that sit neatly inside the top and bottom parts of the casing, thus acting as a 'bridge'.

ⓚ KEY POINT

It is obvious, during these discussions about setting up, that there are some quite critical nuances to the tuning of a bandsaw. It is important to recheck all settings once done, in case anything has changed. Smaller bandsaws perform better when used by a single operator who takes care of the machine. Larger machines will cope with much more punishment and multiple users.

Routine maintenance

Overall good care of your machine is important, as
it will provide a safer working environment, prolong
machine life, and you will be more familiar with
the specific settings needed on your machine.

With the better-quality machines, there should
be less initial setting up and theoretically less
maintenance needed, but it makes good sense to
have some kind of routine programme of ongoing
checks to ensure that the machine is working to
maximum efficiency. The following checklist will
help to keep a semblance of order in this sometimes
tedious aspect of woodworking:

Blade removal and changing

1 Firstly and importantly, isolate the machine from
   the power supply.
2 Open the top and bottom bandwheel doors by
   turning the knobs or handles provided.
3 Detach the fence bar that is usually fitted to the
   front of the table.
4 Remove the bolt or setscrew that is located in the
   front of the table edge for holding the two parts
   of the surface flush.

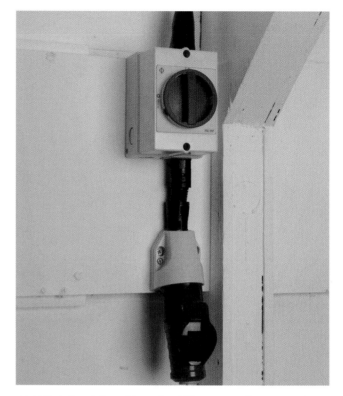

**ABOVE Industrial machines should have an isolation switch
either on the machine, or on the wall as in this case. Domestic
machines must have the plug taken out of the wall socket.**

**BELOW Fence-bar fixings usually consist of bolts or knobs and
are sometimes awkward to reach.**

5 Turn the tension knob anticlockwise to release the blade tension. Newer models may have a quick-release blade-tension lever.

LEFT When removing any nuts, bolts and washers, run the nuts and washers back on to the detached bolts so you don't lose any parts.

BELOW LEFT Always release the tension fully so the whole mechanism gets a chance to 'work' and does not get stiff from being at one setting.

BELOW The quick-release lever has been pulled to the left to detension the blade. Note how the tension knob on top has dropped down to case level.

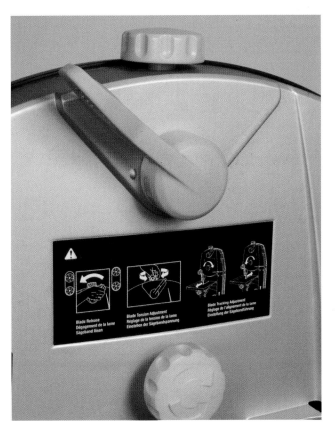

6 Remove the bandsaw blade by feeding it through the upper blade guides and guard, and the slot in the table. Take care not to cut yourself – wear gloves, if necessary.

7 Check the tracking on the newly fitted blade by turning the upper wheel by hand. The blade should run as close to the centre of the bandwheel as possible.

8 If required, adjust the tracking using the tracking knob and lock knob to the rear of the upper bandwheel housing. When the tracking is correct, lock the setting.

9 Reset the blade guides.

10 Close and lock both the bandwheel doors before reconnecting the power supply.

11 Finally, the blade tension indicator is a guide only and may need recalibrating periodically.

LEFT Handling blades is safer with work gloves but it is usually quite difficult trying to ease the blade out of the case, so finger with care.

(FOCUS ON:

Blade changing on quick-release machines

For quick-release models only: if the new blade being fitted is a different width to the one being removed, before the new blade is placed around the bandwheels you should:

1 Reapply the quick-release lever, moving the bandwheel upwards, and adjust the tension wheel to suit the new blade size (don't over-tension when choosing a setting for a blade size you haven't installed before).

2 Once the tension indicator is showing the correct reading for the new blade, release the cam handle and place the new blade on the bandwheels. (If you have a standard machine without quick release, leave the tension off until this point.)

3 When fitting the new blade, ensure the blade teeth are pointing downwards and towards you at the position where the blade passes through the table.

4 Ensuring that the blade is fully in place on the bandwheel, re-apply tension using the quick-release lever (increase tension using the tension knob if using a conventional machine).

5 Fine-adjust the blade tension further if required, using the blade-tension knob.

Alternatively, if the new blade width is the same as the blade being removed:

1 Fit the new blade, ensuring the teeth are pointing downwards and towards you at the position where the blade passes through the table.

2 Ensure that the blade is fully in place on the bandwheel: reapply tension using the quick-release lever.

3 Fine-adjust the blade tension further if required, using the blade-tension wheel.

KEY POINT

Use silicone spray for lubricating the blade guides, not oil or grease, which would attract dust and cause the rollers to jam.

Drive belt replacement

To replace the drive belt, first undo the nut on the hub, using the correct-size ring or socket spanner (wrench), and remove the lower bandwheel. Then simply loosen the tension on the belt by the means provided (often this is a lock lever, to slacken off the motor), remove the old belt and fit the new one. Once the drive belt is in place, refit the lower bandwheel and tighten the nut (grip the wheel rim to apply pressure against the spanner). Now tension the drive belt by adjusting the motor position according to the machine manual until the belt is taut (slight depression by finger pressure on the flat of the belt is correct).

BELOW Wipe up any surplus spray, as it will mark your work, which will need degreasing as a result.

Guide assembly maintenance

Before replacing components on the guide assemblies, ensure that the blade is removed. Once the guards are removed, the various components can be accessed and replaced. Undo the relevant hex nuts for either the guide rollers or rear thrust pad, and fit the new parts. Once the new components are fitted the blade should be refitted and the guides adjusted accordingly.

If you only need to replace the roller bearings on either side, or the thrust roller bearing at the rear, then simply undo the relevant screw or bolt and replace the part. When the new components are in place, the blade should be refitted and the guides adjusted to the correct tolerances as previously discussed.

SAFETY

Make it a habit before carrying out any adjustments or maintenance to ensure that the machine is isolated and disconnected from the electricity supply.

Table insert

The table insert on a bandsaw is a consumable item which will need replacing periodically. To carry out this procedure, simply push the old insert out from underneath the table and fit the new one in position. It is easier still if the blade is not in place, but this is not strictly necessary.

Bandwheel tyres

The bandwheels on most machines have rubber tyres fitted to the outer rim, to protect the set of the blade when in use, to provide traction and to stop the blade slipping. As part of your regular service schedule, inspect the tyres for wear and damage, and replace if necessary. If tyres are worn, tracking the blade will be much more difficult, even impossible, so changing the tyres will become necessary. Simpler bandwheels may just have a self-adhesive cork band stuck on the rim; others may have a removable rubber tyre.

To replace a rubber tyre, first remove the blade from the bandsaw, then remove the bandwheel. Gently ease the existing tyre from the rim, taking care not to damage the bandwheel; these are often cast aluminium – a fairly soft material – on lower priced models and permanent damage can be inflicted on the wheel if you are not careful. It will help to have a couple of small tyre irons (available from any motorcycle shop) or even a large flat-headed screwdriver to ease the old tyre off. Gently lever up the tyre from the wheel by inserting the first tyre iron, from that point insert the other tyre iron and slowly work your way around until the tyre comes away.

Heating the new tyre first in hot water will soften the rubber and make it easier to stretch over the bandwheel. Replacement tyres are much smaller than the bandwheel and a good deal of stretching is required to make them fit. It is therefore advisable to have the help of a second person to stretch the new tyre on to the wheel. If not, use a 'C' clamp to grip the tyre in place as you manoeuvre it onto the outer rim of the wheel.

The glued-on cork type, however, needs a lot of laborious scraping with a chisel or something similar, and a good cleaning to remove all glue and cork bits. Use white spirit (mineral spirit) as a solvent with a kitchen scourer pad (exercising care when handling it, as it is inflammable, gives off a vapour that should not be inhaled and can cause skin burns!).

Bandwheel bearings

These are sealed-for-life units which will need replacing only very rarely if at all, unless the bandsaw is used industrially. When replacing the bearings, remove the hex-head bolt from the hub and the bandwheel. You will notice that there are two separate bearings fitted in the hub, pressed up against each other. Take a drift, wide flat-headed punch or similar, and tap one of the bearings out, then push out the second bearing. To fit the new bearings, position by hand in the wheel hub and tap in gently and evenly until the bearing seats against the ridge in the casting.

Cleaning the table

The best bandsaw tables are ground from cast iron and, if cared for properly, will provide smooth and accurate performance. Equally, though, rusting can occur easily, so do not put tea mugs on the surface, as ring marks will result. Obviously, when machining wood a certain amount of resin will be deposited on the surface, and to ensure optimum performance the table needs to be properly cleaned at regular intervals. First, brush off all loose particles, then wipe clean with white spirit, ensuring that any resin

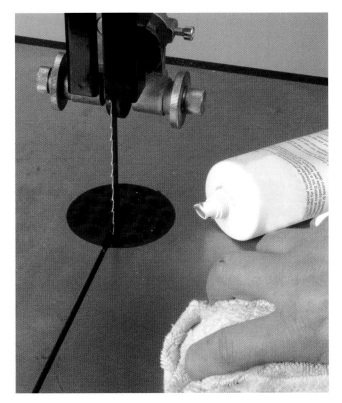

ABOVE This is a special machine-bed wax with added graphite, but any good-quality water-free furniture wax, especially the sort that hardens off, will do.

build-up is dispersed and removed, if necessary using a paint scraper to remove lumpy resinous accretions. Once the table has been thoroughly cleaned it can be treated with a silicone spray or non-water-based wax. If these guidelines are followed, the timber will glide smoothly and easily across the table.

The bandwheel brush

The purpose of this brush is to remove any excess sawdust and resin from the bandwheel and tyre. If it isn't present, deposits can build up on the lower wheel and cause erratic performance. The brush will need adjusting periodically.

Before each use inspect the brush and make sure it is making sufficient contact with the bandwheel to remove sawdust from the tyre (it should be

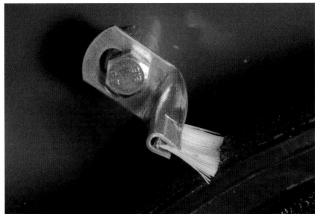

ABOVE The bandwheel brush is essential, and it should have a degree of adjustment to maximize its cleaning ability. Resinous wood, however, will stick to the tyres and will need to be scraped off by hand.

touching – but not applying pressure to the wheel). If necessary, loosen the fixing and adjust so that it makes contact with the wheel. When the bristles are worn, and the brush cannot be adjusted any nearer the wheel, it must be replaced.

Periodically the brush may also become clogged up with resin – especially when cutting a long run of softwood. If this occurs, the resin must be scraped or soaked off with white spirit as the performance of the brush will be reduced.

Lubrication

The following parts of the bandsaw should be lubricated periodically – preferably using powdered graphite, as oil or grease attract sawdust, whereas dry, powdered graphite will not. The downside of using graphite, especially to excess, is that it will deposit dark marks on timber, hands and everything else present, so use it sparingly on the following:

- the blade-tensioning screw inside the cover
- the square upper blade-guide post
- the upper and lower blade-guide adjusting screws
- the table-tilt trunnion.

To grease the upper wheel bearings

1 Remove the upper-wheel shaft retaining ring and washer.
2 Wipe the shaft with a clean rag to eliminate dust and dirt.
3 Apply a minute amount of any suitable grease such as automotive bearing grease, cup grease, or furnace-bearing grease.
4 Replace all components.

Cleaning

As you work with your bandsaw, fine sawdust will dry out bearings and cause them to wear prematurely, and pitch will accumulate on the tyres, blade guides and blades, affecting your machine's performance. If you use a stiff-bristle brush and mineral spirits (discarded 'firm' toothbrushes are ideal for this), it is quite easy to remove impacted dust from those regions. Regular vacuuming out of the case will help deal with the prodigious build-up of sawdust.

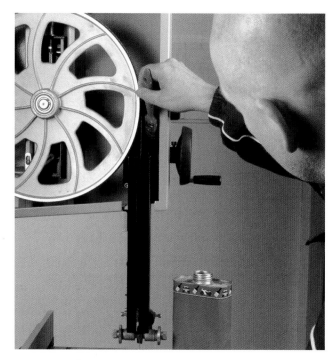

ABOVE Brushing on a degreasing agent.

'As-required' maintenance

Blade sharpening

Your blades will eventually dull to the point where they will have to be sharpened or replaced. Unless you are lucky enough to have the equipment to do this, they should go to a saw doctor for resharpening. Bear in mind, though, that the blade width will reduce slightly and the cost may not make it an economic proposition, especially for small or narrow blades. Sadly, it is usually better to throw worn blades away. A good plan is to have several blades in stock, keeping the newish ones for 'best' and the part-worn ones for coarse work. If they are the same width, blade changeover becomes relatively quick if you want to swap them according to the grade of work being done.

Resurfacing guide blocks

Through use, the guide blocks on your bandsaw will become worn or scored. To resurface the guides to their original shapes, you can use a flat-surfaced grinding or sanding tool such as a belt sander, strip sander, disc sander, or a whetstone if they are the metal type. However, as they are quite small, handling them safely may mean creating a small jig to hold them, if for no other reason than avoiding the resultant heat build-up. In any case wood guide blocks are best made from scratch as a long strip, then cut down to the right length.

> **KEY POINT**
>
> When resurfacing guide blocks it is important that you maintain their current angles and remove as little material as possible in the process. The blocks need to be long enough to clamp in the guide-block holders while still projecting enough to touch the blade.

Maintenance schedule

A routine maintenance schedule should be drawn up to include, for example: blade condition, pulley-bearing wear, pulley wear, correct operation of guides and thrust wheels, blade tensioning device, blade and pulley cleaning equipment, guards and safety devices.

Blade care

Before blades are used again, check for wear, damaged teeth and cracks. This will not take long and should become an automatic operation when repeated a few times. It will save time in the long run rather than having to change blades mid-cut when you discover the teeth are not in a fit condition.

KEY POINT

Never clean the blade or wheel with a hand-held brush or scraper while the blade is in motion. Hold the blade and scrape the wheel while turning it with the power off. Careful adjustment and regular maintenance of blade and pulley-cleaning equipment should help ensure resin residues do not build up.

FOCUS ON:

Routine maintenance and cleaning

- Every five hours of running time, brush or blow out the bandsaw completely.

- Every ten running hours, repeat previous steps and, in addition, check all alignments and adjustments.

- Every 20 hours clean all pitch from blades, blade guides and tyres. Lubricate the trunnions, blade-tension screw, blade, guide post and blade-guide adjusting screws. Coat the table surface, the mitre-gauge slot and the table insert with a high-quality furniture wax or silicone spray, and buff off. This will help your workpieces glide more easily and smoothly across the surface during operations, and protect metal surfaces from rust formation.

- Every 50 running hours, repeat previous steps and, in addition: grease the wheel bearings, check all guide blocks or guide bearings and tyres for wear.

ABOVE Whether a used blade is going blunt or still has service life ahead, make sure you use something like wire ties or cable ties to hold the blade neatly once folded. This avoids personal injury and unnecessary damage to the teeth as well.

1:4 Blades

Many people still consider the bandsaw to be a machine for cutting curves only, and of course bandsaws are unequalled for sawing stock into circles or intricate shapes. However, a correctly set-up saw will make straight cuts through thick material with equal ease, both safely and efficiently. The correct choice and use of blade, in addition to proper setting up of the machine, allows the bandsaw to fulfil its full potential as a creative woodworking machine.

It is never wise to rely on just one or two blades. The time that you are most likely to need a new blade, perhaps through breakage or excessive blade wear, is when you are in the middle of a critical operation. Only a few of the more unusual blade sizes need to be kept in stock, but always keep a supply of 'standard' blades handy in case of need.

Blade types

Modern bandsaw blades are made from toothed strips of hardened and tempered carbon steel, usually joined by a flash-butt welding process. There are three basic types:

File-sharpened blades

These are the original type, without the advantage of hardened teeth, available in a range of pitches but with triangular-shaped teeth only. File-sharpened blades are difficult to obtain as they have largely been superseded by the hardened-tooth type, but they still have some dedicated adherents who believe they are superior to the newer, hardened variety. Because the teeth are softer, the blades need to be run further forward on the bandwheels; this prevents the 'set' of the blades being lost due to the tension of the bandwheels and the resultant pressure when the teeth are sitting right on the tyre camber. Running narrow blades right at the front edge of a fast-moving bandwheel, with the teeth overhanging the wheel, is not something most people should try, as it takes care, skill and nerves of steel!

It is possible to sharpen these blades by hand filing, but it is a demanding task and likely to give a poor result unless done by an expert. However, if you wish to have a go at hand filing, use a tapered, round-cornered file held to give a 100° hook angle. Cracks can start at a sharp internal corner in the gullet, so use bigger files with more rounded corners for large pitches and smaller ones only for short pitches – in both cases with the file roughly half as wide again as the tooth back.

After filing, bandsaw teeth need setting to restore the original kerf (cutting width). Setting is the process of bending tooth points to right and left alternately, to give working clearance and allow the blade to saw in straight and curved lines, without binding in the cut. Setting is possible using a narrow hammer or a hand-operated plier-type saw set, but is much faster using a dedicated machine setter.

Set on a bandsaw blade makes the cutting or kerf width wider than the thickness of the blade body by up to a maximum of ⅓₂in (0.75mm). More set is needed for wide blades and for cutting softwood, while less is needed for narrow blades and for cutting hardwood and composite boards. File-temper bandsaw blades can be sharpened and reset any number of times but, while some tooling companies will still file and set bandsaws of this type, fewer are now willing to do this.

ABOVE Before the advent of modern, hardened bimetal blades, running a blade on the crown of the tyre like this was not acceptable because the teeth would lose their set. Instead the blade would be run rather precariously with the teeth overhanging the front edge.

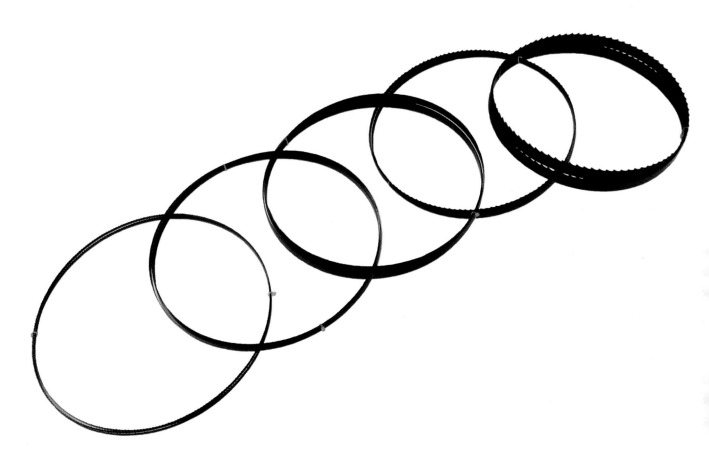

ABOVE A typical selection of bandsaw blades.

(FOCUS ON:

Obtaining bandsaw blades

Just as it is difficult to find local machinery or tool dealers where you can buy bandsaws in person, so it can be difficult to find a local supplier for bandsaw blades, and in any case often they will not have the one you want in stock. They may offer to order the blade and ring you when it is in, but this isn't acceptable, as you do not necessarily know what you are buying without seeing it in person.

Almost always it is better to buy by mail order or online from a specialist supplier (see 'Resources', on page 170) who will keep every type and size in stock ready to go, off the shelf. You should be able to choose between skip and non-skip-tooth types (see page 78) and the precise number of teeth per inch that you need. Pay by credit or debit card and you will get fast delivery – much faster than your local shop.

Flexi-backed hardened-tooth blades

This is the most popular type of bandsaw blade, manufactured in various pitches and with a choice of tooth styles: triangular for metal and fine wood cutting – cutting in thin ply, and so on – and skip-tooth (like a triangular tooth, but with alternate teeth removed) for heavier timber and composite boards. Fine-pitch saws can have wavy-set teeth, which are suitable for metals, and will usually cut thin plastic with little break-out. Medium and coarse-pitch saws usually have teeth set to right and left alternately. For faster cutting, however, teeth may be set raker fashion, in groups of three teeth: two alternately set teeth and the third without set.

Because the teeth are hardened, the blades can be set back on the bandwheel so the teeth are higher up the tyre camber, as the teeth will not be deformed by the tensioned blade running further back on the tyre.

Bimetal is another – more costly – hardened-tooth type, with high-speed steel welded to the tips during manufacture. This type is used mainly for non-woodworking applications.

Broken saws can be rejoined, but the cost of this must be balanced against whatever life remains in the saw. Also the length must be checked, as rejoining a saw shortens it, and it may become too short for use. Although less bandsaw-blade length is

ABOVE This wide blade is perfect for straight or deep cutting but would not suit everyone's needs.

lost by butt-welding than the previous lap-brazing method, this process still shortens the blade. Most users consider it more convenient and cost-efficient to replace dull or broken hardened-tooth blades rather than continually refurbishing file-tempered ones, as the quality of work will then also be higher and much more consistent.

Both types of blade are made in different thicknesses (or gauges) and widths. They are manufactured in large coils with teeth already ground and set, and are simply butt-welded to whatever length is needed. Most users will buy the blades already cut and brazed to length for their type of machine. Industrially, blades may be made up on site to suit each machine in a big workshop.

> **◉ KEY POINT**
>
> All hardened-tooth blades are classed as throwaway. Whilst they can possibly be reground, the teeth are too brittle to be reset. To offset this, though, before they become too dull to use they have a much longer life than file-tempered blades.

Carbide-tipped blades

Tungsten-carbide-tipped (TCT) blades are now available for bandsaws as they are for most other machines. Bearing in mind the number of tips that have to be brazed on and ground to profile, this is an expensive alternative to hardened blades. However, where a lot of throughput is required – e.g. when working with hardwoods, especially with natural silica inclusions, or cutting lots of manmade board such as MDF – it makes more economic sense. These are mainly practical on wider blades, with plenty of blade body to support the TC tips.

⊙ FOCUS ON:

Stock blades

It is quite natural to be reluctant to spend lots of money on blades, and buying a number of them can be expensive. However, your bandsaw won't run without blades and, if you blunt your best, most-used blade – or, more unusually, you break one – then you may end up using an inappropriate one, such as a narrow blade for deep cutting, or a ply-cutting, non-skip-tooth blade for solid wood.

When you first acquire a bandsaw it is a good idea to buy a selection of blades in different widths and tooth combinations, say ¼in (6mm), ⅜in (9.5mm), ½in (12mm) and ⅝in (16mm) – just one of each, and see which work best for you. Once a standard is established, buy some more of that size. After all, if you like doing intricate cuts in ply rather in a scrollsaw fashion, then ¼in (6mm) blades would probably suit you; a lot of resawing needs ⅝in (16mm) or even ¾in (19mm) sizes; while the rest of us would settle for either ⅜in (9.5mm) or ½in (12mm) skip-tooth blades. Only experiment and regular use will show what is best for you.

RIGHT Close-up of TCT blade. Note the different tooth form and gullet shape. This is because of the different manufacturing methods for TCT blades compared to regular ones.

Different blades for different jobs

Blades are distinguished by two characteristics: the number of teeth per inch (tpi), and the width of the blade.

For a medium coarseness, and as a good general purpose blade, 6tpi is a good size. Larger teeth (fewer tpi) will give you a more aggressive cut, but this isn't always best.

To understand the difference, imagine cutting down a tree using a wood saw, or doing the same job with a steak knife. The steak knife has very small teeth or no teeth at all, while the wood saw has large teeth. A tree could be cut down with a steak knife, but it would be difficult: the teeth simply aren't aggressive enough.

Equally, a steak can be cut with a wood saw but, even though the wood saw has aggressive teeth, we know it isn't the right blade for the job. Imagine what making this cut would be like: it would probably take only one stroke, but it would be a difficult stroke. The large teeth would dig in and all the force normally exerted over several strokes would be needed all at once. So even though it would be faster, it would be more difficult.

Now think of what is happening to the blade. As the force pushing the saw is increased, the force on each of the teeth is also increased. At some point this force can become too great and damage the blade, either by causing it to be dulled or by actually breaking teeth off. This wouldn't happen when cutting a steak, of course, but this can be a problem with harder materials.

In any cutting job, you want each tooth to be doing a small amount of work. This will keep the force on the teeth light and prevent wear on the blade. But having too few teeth will make cutting impossible. Choosing the proper blade involves making trade-offs.

FACING PAGE A selection of blades running the whole gamut from fine-toothed ply-cutting blades to deep ripping skip-tooth blades.

BELOW A fine-tooth ply-cutting blade.

A moderately fine blade.

An 8tpi skip-tooth blade.

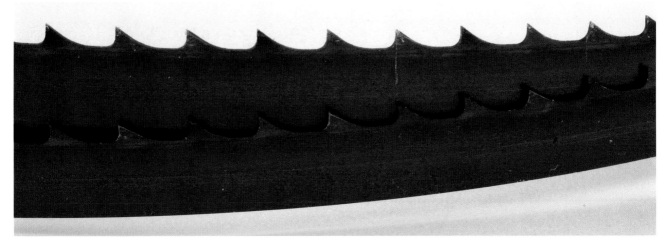

A 6tpi skip-tooth blade.

A 4tpi skip-tooth blade.

Selecting a blade

To achieve optimum cutting performance, it is important to choose the best blade configuration. This is primarily dependant on two factors: material thickness and material type.

- For wood, aluminum, and brass: use the biggest teeth possible to avoid clogging. These materials are soft enough to avoid damaging the blade.
- For tubes, use small teeth: when cutting round materials, the teeth will grab at the side of the piece and try to turn it; smaller teeth make this less of a problem.
- For sheet material, use small teeth: with thin pieces it's easy to get the piece caught in between the teeth, so that all the force is concentrated on one tooth – finer, non-skip-tooth blades prevent this.

Teeth per inch (tpi)

Bandsaws are available with teeth of different pitches, from a fine pitch of about $\frac{3}{16}$in (5mm), to a coarse pitch of about $\frac{9}{32}$in (7mm). Generally pitch is classified as the number of 'teeth per inch' (most commonly 4–10tpi). Fine-pitch saws are used for thin, hard and brittle materials, coarse pitches for deep cutting and softer materials.

Greater tpi should be selected as material thickness decreases but, if the tpi is too great, the tooth loading will be insufficient to enable penetration and cutting. The teeth will also rapidly lose their sharpness.

For thicker material a lower tpi should be used, otherwise the gullets between the teeth will not be sufficient to clear the waste and the blade will stall, or burn the wood.

It is generally accepted that skip-tooth blades give the fastest, most accurate cut in thick material, as they remove waste quickly without clogging.

The 'Blade Selection Table' opposite gives guidance on the tpi that should achieve the best results when cutting a variety of material types and thickness. However, it is a guide to selection only. Exact tooth configurations are not always available, nor are all blade configurations covered, but the principles remain the same. Please note that over 25mm or 1inch thickness the 3–4tpi blade is standard for most purposes.

ABOVE A good standard ½in (12mm) blade with skip teeth can be used for most purposes.

BLADE SELECTION TABLE

Material	Material thickness			
	¼in (6mm)	¼–½in (6–12mm)	½–1in (12–25mm)	1in (25mm)
Perspex	16tpi	14tpi	–	–
Chipboard	–	6tpi	3–6tpi	3–4tpi
Fibreboard	16tpi	14tpi	–	–
Hardboard	10tpi	–	–	–
Plywood	10tpi	8tpi	6tpi	3–4tpi
Strawboard	14tpi	10tpi	–	–
Cork	14tpi	6tpi	3tpi	3–4tpi
Leather	14tpi	–	–	–
Rubber	10tpi	8tpi	–	–
Wood – log	–	–	–	3–4tpi
Wood – soft	6tpi	3–6tpi	3–4tpi	3–4tpi
Wood – hard	6tpi	3–6tpi	3–4tpi	3–4tpi
Wood – wet	–	–	–	3–4tpi

Blades of 8tpi or coarser are normally of skip-tooth configuration

ⓀEY POINT

When cutting thin materials they make a very loud, piercing sound, which can drown the normal running sound of your machine. Wear ear and eye protection as usual, but do not allow this higher noise level to mask any other unusual noises that your machine might make if it has developed a fault. Between cuts, check that the bandsaw is still running normally.

Blade thickness

Blade thickness is dictated by the diameter of the bandwheel fitted to the bandsaw. Those ready-made for standard machines will be correct, but the thickness for others is determined by the supplier, from their overall length. Longer blades are obviously used on machines with large-diameter bandwheels, so can be thicker and stronger. Shorter blades are used on machines with smaller-diameter bandwheels and must be thinner, or they may crack in use.

⦿ KEY POINT

Narrow blades are less able to resist normal cutting stresses, so always use the widest blade suitable for the smallest radius to be sawn.

Blade width

Bandsaw blades are offered in popular widths from ¼–1⁹⁄₁₆in (6–40mm). Narrower ones than ¼in (6mm) are available, but are not really suitable for regular use. The narrowest blades are used for sawing curves of small diameter, wider ones for straight cuts and curves of larger diameter. Blades in all cases should be narrower than their bandwheels, so wider blades are restricted to industrial machines.

When cutting shapes, the width of the blade limits the minimum radius that can be cut. If the blade is too wide for the cutting radius, it will twist and possibly jam or break. The smaller the radius, the narrower the blade has to be. Because makers' standards vary, no overall guide can be given for the blade width relative to the minimum curvature it will cut. To select the correct width of saw blade, measure the smallest radius of any curve to be cut, then choose the widest blade that will cut this curve

ABOVE The large size of this bandwheel means that the blade metal does not get stressed. It can, therefore, be thicker than blades used on smaller machines.

without bending. Excessive blade twisting can easily cause a blade to break. With a blade about ½in (12mm) wide, it is possible to cut a curve with a radius of about 3in (76mm). For most purposes a blade width of ⅜–½in (9–12mm) will suffice for general bandsawing, but very tight curves will therefore obviously need a much narrower blade.

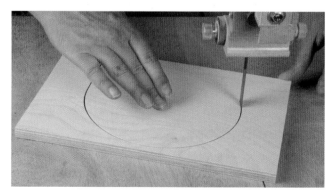

ABOVE Cutting a small-diameter circle requires a slightly narrower blade to avoid it jamming in the cut.

Correct cutting technique

Having selected an appropriate blade for the particular thickness and type of material to be sawn, it is essential that too much pressure is not applied, as that would prevent the blade from cutting freely. If excessive pressure has to be applied, it is probably because of incorrect blade selection or a worn blade, resulting in inaccurate cutting and possibly blade breakage. The tooth pitch should be chosen to suit the material thickness. The rule is, have at least three teeth in the material being cut. The tooth form should suit the material being sawn, so use a skip-tooth blade for natural timber. Follow the manufacturer's recommendations.

Calculating blade length

To work out the blade length required when a replacement is needed, you can simply measure the old one. However, if you prefer to work this out mathematically, for two-wheel bandsaws the following procedure can be followed:

1 Adjust the wheels to their correct position (about the middle of the adjustment range). Ensure the wheels are not adjusted to their extremes, as you need to allow for take-up to tension the band and also for possible future blade rewelding.

2 Measure the distance between the centre point of each wheel (call this measurement D).

3 Now measure the radius of each wheel (R1 and R2).

4 Use this formula to calculate the band length from the measurements you have taken: band length = $(R1 \times 3.1416) + (R2 \times 3.1416) + (2 \times D)$.

ABOVE An original and very discreet blade joint. If a blade snaps and is still usable, it is possible to have a small section removed and then rejoined by a saw doctor using specialist brazing equipment.

FOCUS ON:

Folding a bandsaw blade

1 Hold the blade in front of you with one hand, with the teeth pointing away from you and your foot inside the loop. Step on the blade, securing it firmly to the floor.

2 Then simultaneously rotate and lower your hand as you hold the top of the blade.

KEY POINT

Once unfolded, make sure that the blade has not been turned inside-out – the teeth should point downwards on the right-hand side. More than one bandsaw user has assumed they had a blade designed for a different machine, just because they had unfolded it the wrong way!

3 By the time your hand makes three-quarters to one full revolution, the blade will have popped into three coils.

4 Success!

SAFETY

When folding and unfolding a blade, wear gloves and practise until you can do it effortlessly.

An alternative method of folding a blade

1 With the saw teeth face up, grip the back edge of the blade with one hand each side.

2 Twist the blade over in opposite directions, so the teeth first point towards one another and then finally downwards. While doing this, raise the blade loop furthest away, and lower the nearest loop.

3 Bring both hands closer to the loop, with one raised part of the blade over the other. At the same time the nearest and furthest loops should move together and over one another, forming the three loops needed.

4 Success! This is much easier to do in practice, than to describe in words.

Once you have folded a blade, tape or wire it closed so it cannot spring open again. Blades can be hung on nails or hooks as long as they are long enough to prevent the blades from falling off.

Unfolding a bandsaw blade

This is tricky and gloves should be worn. Grip the blade firmly and shake it away from you, taking great care as it can spring open in any direction.

Breaking in a new blade

Although this applies far more to metalworking on a bandsaw, breaking in a new blade is an important and all-too-easily forgotten procedure which it is wise to practise when working with wood, too, as it should help prolong the life of the blade and so save money.

To illustrate, think of the tip of a newly sharpened pencil: if you press down with too much pressure the tip will break. Better to begin lightly until the tip is worn in a little, and then exert more pressure later. Similarly with a new bandsaw blade, the new teeth are more likely to break if too much feed pressure is exerted, so apply less than the normal feed pressure for the first 10–20 minutes of cutting, gradually increasing the pressure until you are cutting normally.

Fitting the bandsaw blade

Open or remove the front cover to give full access. Open up the guides, move the thrust wheels and guides clear of the present blade, and remove the table insert. The top wheel, of course, has a tension knob or lever to lower it so that the blade can be placed on both wheels easily. Thread the new blade through the table slot and between the side guides and then place it so that the blade lies centrally on all the wheels.

Raise the top wheel – using the handwheel provided – to give the correct tension to the blade, using less tension for narrow blades and more for wider ones. Most machines incorporate a compression spring, but some use a cushioned counterbalance weight.

BELOW Offer up the blade to both wheels at once.

Use the tension scale, where provided, to set the correct tension – otherwise it is simply a matter of practice and user judgement. As a guide, under-tensioned blades may run badly, or even move across the pulleys when sawing. Over-tensioning gives no visible sign, but puts more strain on the blade and increases the chance of breakage.

Make sure that the blade does not catch on anything: turn the upper bandwheel by hand, so that the saw takes up its regular running position. This usually takes several turns. Unless some alteration has been made to the machine after removing the previous blade, the new blade should settle down to run roughly centrally on the wheels. If it does not, adjust the wheel-tracking movement to make the bandsaw run nearer the front or rear, as necessary, until the blade is centred on the wheels. Do this very carefully until you are satisfied it is running correctly.

Once the running position has settled down, close the doors, replace all guards, then start and almost immediately stop the machine, to make sure that the saw is still running in the same position when powered up. If correct, run it for while and then turn off the power; once it stops, set the guides and thrust bearings, as described on page 35.

ABOVE Retensioning the blade to the specified amount.

ABOVE The massive compression spring is clearly visible.

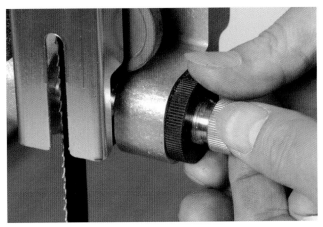

ABOVE Making final guide adjustments before cutting.

Troubleshooting

Problem	Possible causes
Saw blades keep breaking prematurely	Blade tension too high
	Guides tight or maladjusted
	Speed too low for feed rate
	Speed too high
	Cracking at the weld
	Blade too thick for wheel diameter
	Blade pitch far too coarse
Blade starts to camber and cuts to one side, running out of square	Saw guides too far apart
	Feed pressure too high
	Roller guides not adjusted
	Band pitch too fine
	Set removed or reduced by guides
	Blade riding on wheel flange
	Hard inclusion in timber (nails, shot, etc.)
Vibration while cutting	Workpiece not securely held
	Incorrect feed pressure

Problem	Possible causes
Vibration while cutting	Not enough blade tension
	Wrong speed for material
	Pitch too coarse
	Wrong tooth form
Blade dulls prematurely	New blade not run in
	Feed rate too slow
	Speed too high for material
	Pitch too coarse
	Coolant not directed (for metal cutting only)
	Saw idling through cut
	Incorrect saw-guide position for blade width
	Teeth running in wrong direction
	Poor blade quality
Blade twisting	Saw guides too far apart
	Blade binding in cut
	Not enough blade tension
	Blade too wide for radius

Part 2:
Basic Techniques

2:1 Working safely

As with any potentially dangerous woodworking machinery, it is essential to be alert and to use common sense at all times when using a bandsaw. So, despite the possible urge to forego the issue and simply get on with the work as quickly as possible, be ever vigilant and aware of dangers.

The key point about safety is that safe working equals good woodworking practice. In other words, if you adopt good working techniques you are also using safe techniques. Rather than sloppy or ad hoc practices, it is far better to develop standard methods for using the bandsaw and specific bandsaw operations. Additional safety considerations are highlighted in this chapter, which will enable you to stay safe when using the bandsaw.

Bandsaw safety

According to statistics provided by the Health and Safety Executive in the UK, in a recent study of 1000 accidents at woodworking machines only 4 per cent occurred on narrow bandsawing machines. Most of these came from some kind of contact with the moving blade while either pushing material into it or removing material from it. Other accidents occurred when setting, cleaning, adjusting and maintaining the machine while the blade was continuing to rotate, when it should have been stationary.

Many of these accidents could easily have been avoided had the guard been properly in place and a push stick used. Most accidents are due to operator error and checking the machine's set-up is always necessary before starting work.

Familiarize yourself with the regulations in force in your country or state. In the UK, for example, the requirements relating to narrow bandsaws are covered in the *Provision and Use of Work Equipment Regulations* 1998 (PUWER 98) and supported by the *Approved Code of Practice* (ACOP) *Safe Use of Woodworking Machinery* 1998. Machines bearing the CE mark in accordance with the *Supply of Machinery (Safety) Regulations* 1992, should have the guards interlocked with the machine drive (the CE mark is a declaration of conformity for new machines in the European market).

Although the bandsaw feels easy to use and seems relatively safe to cut with, it is sensible to provide a secure auxiliary guard over that portion of the blade which is exposed for cutting purposes, with easy

ABOVE All modern machines have a proper no-volt-release switch like the one shown here. The safety cover allows for quick switch-off and disables the machine when closed.

ABOVE Although this is freehand cutting with the workpiece resting on a narrow edge, the blade is safely covered and the hands are behind the blade line.

adjustment to suit the height of the workpiece. Don't be tempted to ignore Health and Safety guidelines – they provide not only sensible recommendations but also ones which are recognizable in a court of law. So when it is recommended that a safer method be found in order to carry out a certain operation, that advice has legal grounding and, should an accident occur, you may well be culpable or have little course for redress.

If you are not thoroughly familiar with the operation of bandsaws it is worth seeking advice or instruction from a qualified person, so contact your retailer for information on training courses. Be very careful when using a bandsaw until adequate training has been undertaken.

A younger person will need supervision by a suitably qualified operator with a thorough knowledge and experience of the machine and its safeguarding requirements. Anyone supervising must be aware of dangers associated with the operation of the machine, including the following:

- principles of machine operation, correct use and adjustment of the tilting table, fence, jigs, holders, templates and safeguards
- correct selection of saw blade for each operation, set of the teeth, tensioning and tracking
- safe handling of workpieces when cutting
- positioning of hands in relation to the blade
- correct adjustment of the top guide and guard, and of the blade guard below the table
- safe stacking of workpieces before and after cutting.

ABOVE The push block is an underrated method of feeding boards safely.

Siting the bandsaw

A bandsaw with legs that spread for stability is as safe as a freestanding machine can be. A narrow-based bandsaw, however, has quite a small 'footprint' on the floor and, while this is an advantage in that it takes up less room, it could overbalance or turn round if a long, heavy workpiece is rested on it. It should, therefore, be bolted to the floor where possible – permanent fixing might include the use of wedges or pads to level it, large coach screws for wooden floors, or anchor bolts for concrete.

Ensure that there are no serious clashes with other machines, work surfaces, cupboards and so on. Have adequate space, not only to stand at the machine, but also to feed in timber, and have outfeed space where the timber emerges from the machine.

While a woodturner will usually only be cutting out bowl blanks which don't need a lot of space, for cabinetmaking or joinery, long sections will need to be fed at times. Large workshops can use separate work supports for long sections – there are plenty of types on the market, including ball-bearing or roller-topped stands. In a confined situation it might be possible to arrange ingenious outfeed support methods, such as an open window ledge at bandsaw table height, or a block with a roller sitting on the workbench.

ABOVE An assistant can be useful when crosscutting or ripping long lengths.

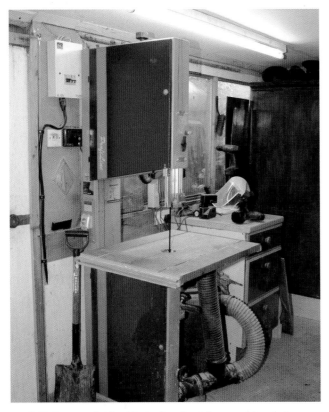

ABOVE A properly sited large bandsaw in a woodturner's workshop, complete with dust extraction from both top and bottom of the lower case.

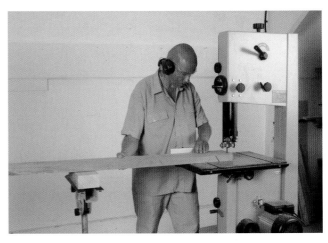

ABOVE A roller stand or other suitable support is invaluable, especially as it increases accuracy as well as safety.

Dust extraction

Unless managed efficiently, dust is a persistent problem for woodworkers. It is both a health hazard and a fire risk, and leads to a very untidy workshop which can be unpleasant to work in.

Bandsaws generate copious amounts of thick rather than fine dust, which settles in the lower part of the case. Quite powerful extraction is therefore needed to shift it, and the best solution is to have a proper extraction unit rather than attempting to improvise.

Workshop extractors can be mobile, fitted under the bench, or wall-mounted. The latter two types are better in a small workshop as they take up less room. A large-bore flexible pipe can be fitted to the machine's own lower outlet and a Y-branch in the pipe rigged up to allow a second, smaller, bore pipe. This can then be fixed near the blade to draw dust away, possibly with the aid of a home-made hood under the table to collect the dust as it drops through.

Generally, the dust produced by a bandsaw is not the most dangerous kind, because the particles are quite coarse (though it can be a problem if you are asthmatic – see page 103). Many woodworkers now use a very fine filtration unit, which can be wall-mounted or hung from the ceiling; this is a very effective way of reducing fine dust in the atmosphere, but it should be used in addition to proper extraction, not as a substitute.

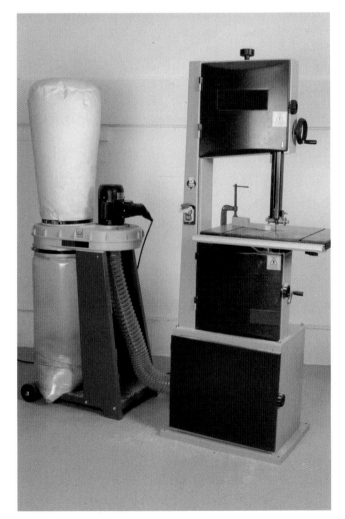

ABOVE A mobile extractor is handy if you want to move it between machines; otherwise, consider a wall-mounted version that will take up less space.

ABOVE A small, wall-mounted air cleaner for removing the very finest and most lethal dust particles. It must be used in conjunction with proper extraction – it is not a substitute.

Safe bandsaw practice

Before using a newly installed machine, and during general operation, observe the following procedures:

1 Ensure the voltage of the machine corresponds to the mains supply voltage.
2 Use a properly earthed power source (wall socket) at all times.
3 The flex and plug must be in good condition, not frayed or damaged. If the mains lead is damaged, it should be replaced by a qualified electrician.
4 Never use a long extension cable – if an extension cable is used, it must be fully unwound.
5 Never turn the machine on before clearing the table of all objects, such as tools, scrap pieces and so on.
6 Never leave the machine running unattended, and do not operate when children or animals are present, or any other sort of distraction or hazard.
7 DO NOT operate the machine with the bandwheel doors open (industrial machines have microswitches to prevent this).

Before getting down to the cutting process, a few other safety checks are necessary, specifically with regard to the blade, which should:

- have no teeth missing
- be in good order, with no cracks or splits
- be the correct type and width for the material being cut
- be set at the correct speed for the material being cut (for most wood cutting applications the faster of the two speeds should be used)
- have sharp teeth which are properly set
- be correctly tensioned and tracked
- be no greater than the maximum thickness suitable for the bandwheel diameter
- have the teeth of the blade pointing downwards for the cut

- have that part of the blade between the underside of the table and the lower guide guarded, no matter what the angle of tilt of the table.

Cutting procedure

The cutting process itself may seem like common sense, but with so many other things to remember it is worth noting that you should:

1 Never start the machine with the blade pressed against the workpiece.
2 Never apply sideways pressure on the blade as this may cause it to break.
3 Always take care when cutting wood with knots, nails or cracks in it and/or dirt on it, as these can cause the blade to get stuck or damaged. Remove foreign objects first where possible.
4 When cutting round timber, use a suitable jig to prevent the workpiece rolling over.
5 Always have guides and guards in the correct position. In particular, ensure the movable blade guard is lowered as close to the workpiece as is practicable.
6 Use push sticks wherever possible; this is especially important with small or narrow pieces (see facing page).

Hand positioning

Your hands are precious, so it is vital to look after them.

- Visualize where your hands are going to be when you have finished a cut as well as where they are at the start position.
- Remember the act of cutting involves pushing the workpiece towards the moving blade, so it is vital that you are aware of where your hands are at all times during the cut.

- When cutting is complete, carefully remove the side cut pieces with a push stick: first the piece which falls away from the blade, then the piece trapped between the blade and the fence. If you don't use a push stick, the machine must be switched off and the blade at a halt before removing pieces near the blade.
- When ripsawing narrow and short pieces, use a push stick in one hand and a spiked stick in the other, spiking the outer edge of the timber to enable it to be moved away safely.
- Never brush offcuts from the saw table with the bandsaw running, unless using a push stick – and even a push stick can get caught on the blade.

Use of push sticks

Always use push sticks if your hands would otherwise be too close to the blade. Make a selection of sticks for various types of work. Easily knocked up from scrap timber, they are disposable but invaluable, and using them regularly is well worth the effort in terms of your own personal safety. (See also page 145.)

Use a push block when deep-cutting timber to produce thin offcuts or wide boards where you need to apply more pressure from behind.

When making a cut, the leading hand must not be closer than necessary to the front of the saw, and hands should never be in the cutting line of the blade. As a rule, if your leading hand reaches the front of the table, use a push stick, or keep your hands to the sides of the workpiece when manoeuvring it onto the running blade.

When removing the wood lying between the blade and the fence after a cutting pass, a push stick should be used, unless the width of the wood exceeds 6in (152mm), in which case it is deemed safe enough to remove by hand.

ABOVE A selection of push sticks, two of which are home-made.

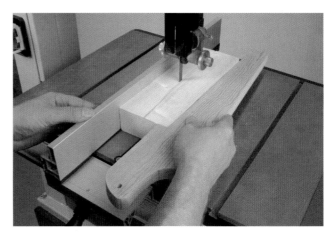

ABOVE A push stick can be used to push down on the work or, as in this case, to apply sideways pressure to keep the workpiece against the fence.

ABOVE A push block is a useful alternative to a push stick, especially for flat boards.

Work support

An essential factor in all operations at the bandsaw is the provision of adequate support. If you are handling larger workpieces, then use extension tables at the infeed, the outfeed and sides of the main table if these are available, in addition to the roller supports mentioned earlier.

In some instances you may choose to use an extra pair of hands to collect the work as it passes through the saw blade. Make sure your assistant is conversant with the workings of a bandsaw, carefully supporting the work without pulling the workpiece through the blade. It is important that an assistant can work almost intuitively with the machine operator, as noise plus ear defenders can make comprehensible speech difficult.

ABOVE How NOT to do it! It is foolish to try a crosscut with a long board like this. The finished cut will be inaccurate because it cannot be guided properly. More importantly, it will cause arm or shoulder strain, and the work is likely to drop down, possibly trapping the blade at full power.

Personal safety

This section is not about the bandsaw, but about you, the operator. Careful regard to how you are dressed and equipped will help protect you and make for a more comfortable and enjoyable experience.

Clothing

Always wear clothing appropriate for a workshop setting:

- loose clothing can be dangerous, especially coats with patch pockets and wide sleeves, both of which can snag on guards, fences and so on
- woodturners' smocks are very practical, with their zip fastening, Velcro cuff straps and pockets at the back (to prevent them filling up with shavings)
- bulky clothing in cold weather restricts movement and must be chosen with care if it is to be safe in use
- loose sleeves should be rolled up above the elbows
- feet should be adequately protected with suitable footwear – such as steel-capped shoes, preferably with non-slip soles – definitely NOT sandals
- long hair should be put in a safety hairnet
- any loose items such as jewellery, medallions on chains and neckties should be removed.

ABOVE A comfortable, reinforced pair of boots with steel toecaps is a worthwhile investment.

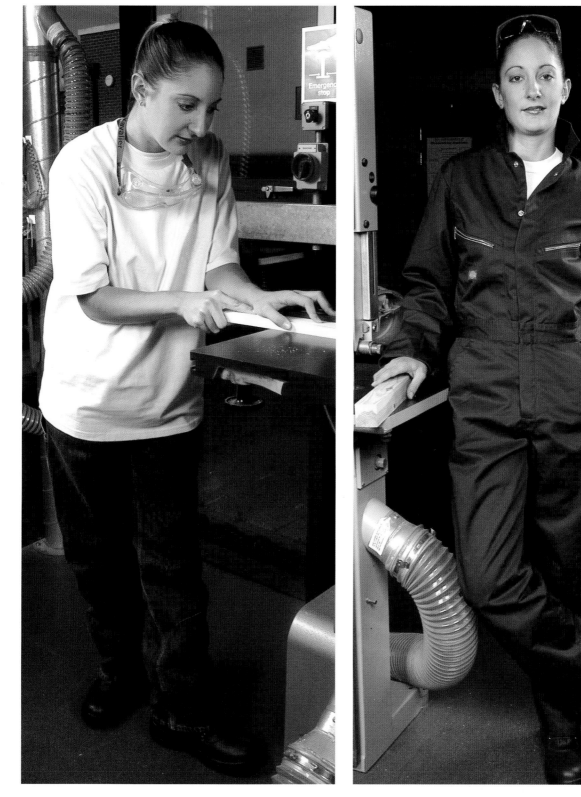

ABOVE A woodworker's smock is a neat solution if you don't mind pockets at the back.

ABOVE A boiler suit definitely isn't just for engineers: it is very practical and helps to keep you warm.

101

Eyewear

Safety eyewear should always be worn, as the eyes are particularly vulnerable to wood or metal particles. Use a pair which will neither fog nor scratch. Some are antistatic, others are tinted, and most wrap fully around the eyes for greater protection from flying debris. All such eyewear should give a degree of impact protection. There are also full-face shields, or full-face respirator masks that both protect the eyes and filter the air, thus avoiding sore eyes as well as giving clean air to breathe.

ABOVE Eye protection can be fashionable – this pair gives wraparound protection and is ventilated to prevent misting.

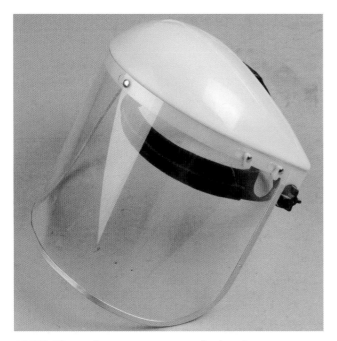

ABOVE Visors often are not very popular, but they are relatively easy to wear as they don't press on the face like goggles. They also flip upwards when not required.

Ear protection

Ear defenders or earplugs will help protect you from hearing loss. Especially recommended are the extremely lightweight hearing bands, less intrusive than standard ear muffs, which can be a little cumbersome and may interfere with safety spectacles or goggles.

Noise levels will vary from machine to machine and depending on the conditions of use. Operators exposed to high noise levels, for even a short time, may experience temporary partial hearing loss. Worse still, exposure to continuous high levels of noise may lead to permanent hearing damage, including the onset of tinnitus.

RIGHT This deluxe pair of headphones offers advanced ear protection. The knob on the side adjusts the level of noise self-cancelling, so that when talking to someone you can hear them. Once a machine starts, normal speech is blotted out as the counter-soundwave protection kicks in. It then switches off soon after the machine noise dies.

ⓘ KEY POINT

The use of an audio headset does not constitute safe working practice! The sound level masks workshop and machine sounds and the wires can get caught on the machine.

ABOVE A standard set of ear defenders giving a good level of protection.

Dustmasks and respirators

Exposure to dust from all wood is hazardous, but some wood dust is worse than others, causing differing levels of skin, eye or breathing irritation, allergic reaction, asthma and even carcinogenic associations. The same applies to dust created by composite materials, such as MDF, and certain plywood laminates.

A range of face masks is available. The simplest type gives only short-time protection before it has to replaced. The moulded sort – which fits round your nose and mouth and has a breather valve – is amongst the most practical.

Masks are classified according to the type of dust they protect against, and can be obtained from the large DIY stores as well as specialist shops. The degree of protection is printed on the packaging. A very effective but expensive way of protecting eyes and lungs simultaneously is with a full-face battery-powered respirator, in which a stream of filtered air is blown down over the face and out at the bottom of the mask. These are excellent for spectacle wearers because they keep your lenses clear (unlike some other types of goggles), and they are very efficient at protecting your eyes from dust exposure. In the long run they are the most complete and effective solution.

ABOVE A full-face powered respirator offers the safest form of lung and eye protection available.

ⓈSAFETY

Stay alert

Above all, watch what you are doing. Apply common sense and do not use the machine when you are tired. Don't let yourself be distracted and, if you feel the onset of tiredness or your attention wandering, take a break and a rest. That way you can avoid accidents.

ABOVE This relatively simple mask, slightly more sophisticated than the basic 'monkey mask', takes replaceable filter liners.

ABOVE It is good to break concentration deliberately: sit down if you've been standing, read a novel instead of doing calculations, or go for a walk and some fresh air.

General workshop safety

ABOVE There is plenty of room to use this bandsaw but not a lot of outfeed space, because it is used by a woodturner cutting bowl blanks. A cabinetmaker would need a lot more space to the right of the table. Note the compact extractor.

Ideally, a workshop should be clean, well ordered and tidy, but all too often this is not the case. In domestic workshops woodworking may share space with other things, such as a car in a garage, or lots of domestic clutter in a shed. And, if you have the luxury of space and money, there is the temptation to buy lots of kit that fills the space and renders it effectively unusable for constructing a project.

Workshop layout

Plan out the workshop space on paper, taking account of the bench, bandsaw, shelves, door, window and any other major items. Allow room to carry out all likely woodworking operations, including infeed and outfeed to the bandsaw. You can then put this paper plan into action and hopefully have a usable and safe workshop as a result.

Heating and electrics

Plenty of power outlets and lighting are essential, as is a suitable, safe form of heating for a dusty environment.

The light level must be adequate for working and, in particular, the bandsaw and any other machines may need additional lighting on the working area – an anglepoise lamp is effective, but there are other worklights on the market.

Heating must be fully enclosed; oil-filled radiators are suitable, but they only give background heating and really need to be left switched on for some time to be effective. The electrical circuit must be strong enough to cope with the likely combined power loading in the workshop. All cables need to be in ducting for their protection.

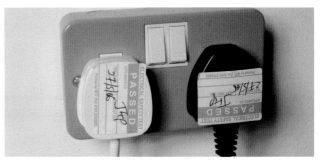

ABOVE Steel-clad wall sockets with buried wiring or surface conduit are safer than standard bakelite, which can get broken. Note the UK PAT test labels. All appliances in commercial or public environments must be tested annually.

ABOVE A fully enclosed oil-filled panel heater is safe and gives background heating in the winter.

ABOVE A wall isolator – rather than a 13amp plug and socket – is required for heavy machines using industrial plugs, especially if a machine is 'hard-wired'.

A tidy workshop

Having created a functional and safe workshop, keep it that way. Cluttered areas and benches invite accidents and injuries. Always sweep up at the end of a work session and dispose of unusable small offcuts. Store any chemicals safely, especially flammable ones. When not in use, tools should be stored in a dry, locked place, out of reach of children.

Safety of visitors

Do not allow children, or anyone not involved in the work, to touch machines or tools, and keep visitors away from the work area. Impress on anyone visiting the workshop that it is a work area and they are at risk if they touch or handle anything.

ABOVE A fire extinguisher is essential. Choose one suitable for use with live electrics. If a fire occurs and one extinguisher won't put the fire out, get out!

FOCUS ON:

Electric machine safety

Always look after tools and machines:
- Follow instructions for lubrication and changing accessories.
- Inspect machine and power-tool leads periodically and, if damaged, have them repaired by an authorized service facility or qualified electrician. The same applies to extension leads.
- Always use a properly rated extension lead to suit the power tool.
- Never yank the lead to disconnect it from the socket, or pick a power tool up by the lead.
- When not in use – and before servicing, changing blades and so on – disconnect the machine from the power supply.
- If you are not confident about attempting any repairs or maintenance to machines or power tools, have them repaired by a qualified person or appropriate service centre.

ABOVE Modern woodworking machines have sophisticated electrics and electronics which are not generally suitable for user servicing.

First aid

When working with tools and machinery of any kind, you should keep a well-stocked first-aid box readily available, with relevant contact telephone numbers easily accessible. Buy a ready-made kit in a proper case and don't choose the smallest kit – go for a more comprehensive one, as it will be more useful in an emergency. It MUST contain a proper eyewash and eyebath, as minor eye invasion by dust and so on is a common problem in a workshop.

Ⓐ SUGGESTED BASIC FIRST-AID KIT

- Antiseptic ointment
- Antiseptic spray
- Antiseptic wipes
- Good-quality sharp tweezers
  (not to be used on or near the eyes)
- Scissors
- Sticking plasters (wound dressings)
- Butterfly plasters
- Adhesive tape
- Sterile pads of various sizes
- Cold compress
- Eyewash and eyebath
- Mild painkillers
- Sterile gloves
- Safety pins

Remember to replace items as and when required.

ABOVE An eyebath station is essential, as eyes are often unexpectedly vulnerable in a workshop situation.

ABOVE A good-quality, wall-mounted first-aid kit, containing a comprehensive selection of first-aid supplies.

2:2 Basic bandsawing principles

The bandsaw is an excellent machine for ease of use and versatility – whether for complicated cuts and shapes or straightforward rips and curves, but to get the most out of it you need to master the simple techniques outlined in the following pages. They are easy to apply in practice and will give satisfying results every time.

Although this book contains a lot of useful information regarding jigs and other devices, in reality, for a large percentage of work, the bandsaw will be used with nothing more than a straight fence or a mitre gauge and sometimes not even those. The beauty of the bandsaw is its simplicity of use. Being able to walk straight up to a machine and make quick, minor cuts is a positive boon. It is this key feature of the bandsaw that makes it such a desirable asset in the workshop.

First principles

You will find that in a relatively short period of time confidence will grow, as basic – yet still impressive – tasks are completed, such as ripping down wide timber (cutting it along the grain) into narrower strips, cutting out curved legs for a coffee table, or some intricate decorative shaping

Firstly and most importantly there is the need for safety at all times, but there are some other key points to take on board when using the bandsaw. These should become second nature to any serious woodworker.

- The blade cuts on a continuous down stroke, so slowly feed the workpiece towards the blade, using only light pressure and allowing the blade to do the cutting.
- Use a push stick wherever possible and keep your hands well away from the blade.
- For best results the blade must be sharp. Damaged or worn blades should be replaced as soon as possible.
- Select the right blade for the job, depending on the thickness of the wood and the cut to be made.
- For straight cutting use a properly adjusted rip fence.
- When cutting shapes, follow the marked-out design by pushing and turning the workpiece at an even rate. Do not attempt to turn the workpiece without pushing it, as this may cause it to get stuck, or the blade to bend.
- Always plan your cuts to avoid the possibility of a blade jamming: be sure to make escape cuts first, before doing the actual cutting.
- Towards the end of the cut there will be a sudden decrease in resistance, and particular care should be taken to stop hands being thrown into the blade.

- If the blade is already running too far in front of the thrust bearing, due to poor set-up, the blade will spring forward when the cut breaks through, so once again keep fingers well clear of the general blade area.
- Before commencing work on an important project, it is advisable to do some test cuts to check all settings are correct, and try out any jigs or attachments.
- Always ensure that your machine is properly maintained and clean.

ABOVE This is wrong for several reasons: the workpiece is difficult to grip, as it is round and small in diameter; its shape prevents a push stick being used; the final breakthrough is risky, as the blade may spring forward causing a hazard to fingers.

⊙ KEY POINT

Escape cuts are an essential part of good bandsawing cutting practice. It is important to make strategically placed cuts that allow the blade to be released easily when making the main cut or cuts.

Reversing the blade out of a cut

If at all possible, reversing out of a cut should be avoided, as the blade can be dragged off the bandwheels very easily. At the very least, this will bring your cutting session to an abrupt halt and blunt the blade completely as it strikes the inside of the case and the guard. The worst-case scenario is that the blade actually breaks and attacks the operator's hands and arms. Fortunately, the blades in narrow-blade bandsaws – which concern us here – lose their momentum very quickly, so this is a rare event. Large-scale industrial saws are an entirely different matter, as the blades are huge, and store a lot of kinetic energy which they have to get rid of when they snap.

KEY POINT

Very narrow blades need many more teeth per inch as they are normally used in thin timber or board, wider blades need fewer teeth per inch as they are used to cut much thicker timber.

When scroll-cutting or negotiating awkward shapes it may not be possible to complete a cut, and so the blade must be reversed out and care taken to minimize damage to the work and blade.

ABOVE The holes here are part of the design and have been drilled with supersharp Forstner bits, so this blade isn't going to get stuck. There is also an escape cut already made (arrowed), so the pieces will fall away easily from the blade. Forethought in planning out cuts can help avoid a blade finishing its cut in the middle of board with no way out.

When you really must reverse out of a cut it is advisable to leave the blade running, but take extreme care not to pull the blade off the bandwheel. If you can arrange to have waste areas in your workpiece, then you can run the blade into these and jiggle the workpiece gently – until you have enough space to rotate it – then run back through the cut in the other direction, but this may enlarge the cut. It may be possible to arrange to have large pieces in the middle area of the design that can be cut away and lifted, thus freeing the blade completely, but do not attempt to remove any waste until the machine is switched off and the blade has come to a standstill.

Blade stall

In certain circumstances – when cutting thick or wet timber, for example – the workpiece may close up around the blade and cause it to stall. It can be extremely awkward if you are in mid-cut, possibly with quite a large and heavy section of timber, and the bandsaw jams completely.

Wet timber can trap a blade because, once the wider front edge of the blade with its raked teeth has cut through the wood, the soft, wet cells that make up the wood swell and press against the plain, flat body of the blade.

Cut dry timber can also 'move' when the stresses in it are released by sawing, and the two halves of the freshly cut wood settle themselves in a new and conflicting position relative to the blade. This is quite common, but when it does happen it can be extremely awkward to deal with.

In these circumstances, follow this procedure:

- First, switch off the machine and isolate it.
- Make sure the longest projecting end of timber is supported – on a workstand, for example. (If the blade is in the middle, the timber may lie in perfect balance on the machine's table.)
- Next take a slim timber wedge and push it or tap it with a mallet into the open end of the cut, forcing the wood apart enough to allow you to back the timber off the blade with the machine switched off. It is very much a matter of jiggling the timber up and down to get it to slide free of the blade, but it should eventually do so.

ABOVE This board was left outside and got soaking wet. As a result the kerf has started closing up, straining the motor and bringing the blade to a standstill.

> **TIP**
>
> Have to hand a few timber wedges already cut, in case the blade stalls. The bandsaw is perfect for cutting wedges, provided it doesn't already have a baulk of timber jammed on the blade!

It is sometimes possible to resaw the very same cut without jamming the second time, because the wood has already closed up to its maximum. However, feeling a little nervous and uncertain after the first attempt, many of us would rather not be foolhardy and risk it again. Usually it is possible to turn the timber over instead and cut from the other end. With luck it won't jam and – once the blade meets the existing cut – the wood will just part cleanly.

The problem is that the cuts are unlikely to meet exactly, especially if the workpiece wasn't square to start with, the blade was beginning to go blunt, or it was under a lot of strain and so being pulled off course.

KEY POINT

If your bandsaw – or any other woodworking machine – stalls, always switch off quickly. Some motors are protected by a thermal overload, but in any case the strain on a motor when stalled is dangerous and could damage it. Fortunately modern switches are easy to knock to the 'off' position with a thump of the hand.

To get over the problem, cut over-thickness and clean up afterwards – on a planer-thicknesser, if you have one available.

ABOVE A variety of different-sized wedges are needed for different-sized work. A fine cut like this needs a slim wedge, while resawing needs a much chunkier wedge to keep the kerf (saw cut) open.

Ripping

Although ripping (cutting along the grain) is a standard operation for the bandsaw, several factors need to be right for it to work really well: fence adjustment is critical for preventing the blade from wandering, so too is the use of a sharp blade at the correct tension, and the correct setting of the guides and thrust bearing. Narrow finished strips are often produced when ripping on the bandsaw, and you will need a narrow push stick to remove them safely from alongside the fence safely.

For deep ripping the same applies, but it is also extremely important that the blade is perpendicular to the table. Also, if you want an accurate result at the other end, the stock you are deep-ripping must be planed flat and square beforehand.

Obviously, when resawing – cutting rough-sawn timber into boards ready for planing – the boards do not need to be fully prepared all round in the first

KEY POINT

Setting the exact fence-to-blade distance is unfortunately a matter of trial and error. Any scale on the fence bar is likely to be unreliable. It is better to use a steel rule to measure the distance, or make a short test cut and measure the result.

place, as the planer can take care of that. You will need to cut well oversize to allow for planing down.

Standard ripping does not need a machine with a lot of height under the guides, nor does it need anything higher than the standard fence, whereas deep-ripping does need extra cut height, more power, a very rigid case for the machine, plus a high rip fence, which can be home-made (see pages 157) for a deep rip-fence project. As with all things, the more you spend, the better specified the machine, and the more capable it will be of coping with demanding work.

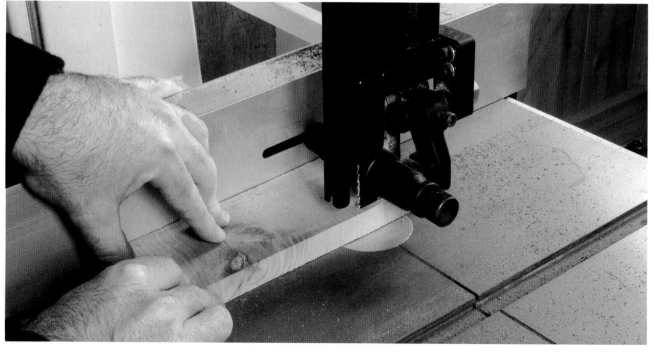

ABOVE A standard rip cut with an accurate blade and fence combination.

Using the mitre gauge

Most bandsaws come with a mitre gauge or protractor that fits in a slot in the machine's table. This is extremely useful and should always be kept handy. Having cut timber to width, you need to cut accurately to length, too. The mitre gauge allows you to do this, and cut mitres (also known as bevel cuts), and can do so in combination with a tilting table to produce what are known as compound mitres, i.e. bevelled in two planes rather than just one.

In order to get the best from a mitre gauge:

1 See that it runs smoothly in the table slot without waggling from side to side – any looseness means it will not give a neat, reliable cut.

2 Check whether it cuts at 90°, by doing trial cuts and testing with an engineer's or combination square. There will be some means of adjustment provided, which may just involve moving the pointer on the protractor scale.

3 Once the 90° setting is confirmed, the other angle settings on the scale should be fine. The test is cutting and fitting together a mitred frame – all four joints must fit neatly together to be acceptable.

4 Having got the accuracy right, you need to fit a wooden subfence on the front face of the mitre gauge. Choose a good, planed, square, flat strip and screw it on. It should lie absolutely flat, so it is perpendicular to the table. Make it long enough to at least reach the table edge – preferably longer – and also to extend a bit beyond the blade at the other end, so that when you take your first cut with it, the blade will trim it to length. That way you will be left with proper support for workpieces right up to the blade.

With bevel cuts, it doesn't matter which way you angle the mitre fence, but the trailing position (angled backwards) does mean that your hand

ABOVE Mitre cutting using a mitre protractor that is supplied with an aluminium subfence.

ABOVE If the mitre protractor is correctly set you will have a perfect 45° mitre joint.

is further away from the blade as you advance the mitre gauge when cutting.

Apart from cutting components to length quickly and neatly, the mitre gauge allows you to do stopped cuts, such as the shoulders of tenons, where you cut to a pre-marked line by eye, or clamp a stop on the table in front of the workpiece for it to come up against, so automatically limiting the shoulder cut. Some mitre gauges have an adjustable length stop, which allows repetition cutting of short pieces to exactly the same length.

> **TIP**
>
> Keep the mitre slot in the table clear of sawdust and regularly wax it along with the table surface, so that the mitre gauge will work smoothly.

Special situations

Cut rotation

The bandsaw column can be a major obstacle to progress with large workpieces. If you need to make a major sweeping cut that is best done in one pass to keep a clean shape, then see if turning the workpiece over might just solve the problem. Simply place your workpiece upside down, mark it out and cut the job upside down. Once the edges are sanded or cleaned up with a rasp it is impossible to tell which way it was cut. Unlike a circular saw, there is little or no grain break-out on the underside.

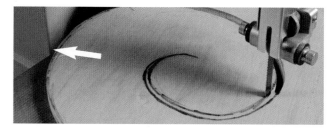

ABOVE Despite careful planning, the tip of this shell design touches the column (arrowed).

Cutting angled components

If you need to angle a workpiece – so it effectively stands on a corner, for instance – hold it in a square carpenter's handscrew or, alternatively, an ordinary clamp and two square blocks of wood. This gives you proper support and control.

ABOVE Cutting two opposing curves with the workpiece angled couldn't be simpler.

Making enclosed cuts

Unlike the scrollsaw, the bandsaw blade cannot be fed through an opening in a blank workpiece to make an enclosed internal cut. The cheat's way around this is to make a cut from outside the workpiece, running with the grain as you enter the inner area to be cut. Once the cut is completed, exit in the same place as neatly as possible so there is just a thin kerf line. Now you should be able to just glue and cramp the kerf closed if there is enough 'give' in the wood, or failing that, cut a thin slip of the same wood and glue and cramp it in the kerf slot. Voilà: a neat invisible joint. Your friends will want to know how you did the cut!

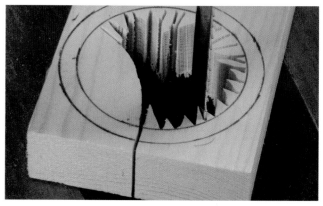

ABOVE The first cuts are tight and quite difficult to negotiate, but it does get easier once some pieces have been removed.

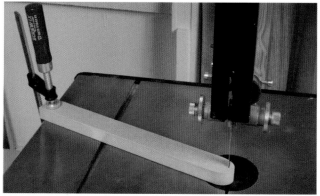

ABOVE The finished item, with a discreet join.

Intarsia work

Joining together different colours and species of wood in a decorative way is referred to as intarsia. Joining irregular-shaped pieces together can be challenging, since the profiles need to match exactly. The technique involves laying one blank above the other, making two identical cuts at the same time, and then joining the opposing pieces of the two different blanks. A refinement, which requires experimentation, is to angle the table slightly, bevelling the edges, so that one piece in effect 'plugs into' the other. This makes for a neat, secure joint. In both cases the edges need to be glued to make a finished joint, which can then be sanded flush afterwards.

ABOVE The stacked, taped halves separated.

ABOVE By tilting the table a 'drop-in' fit is possible.

Mirror cutting

To create a shape that is 'mirrored' from side to side, simply double-tape two blanks together, mark half the design on top and cut both pieces. Clean up the edges, then glue and joint together. With straight grain it is difficult to tell that a join has been made. Since realistically it is difficult for even the best of us to make truly symmetrical shaped cuts, this is the perfect way around the problem.

ABOVE Starting the series of cuts, the short escape cuts having already been made. Double-sided tape ensures the blanks stay together.

LEFT The finished job: once glued and cramped, the joint will be invisible.

2:3 More complex cutting

Having mastered the basics, it would be a shame not to extend the 'performance envelope' of both the bandsaw and you, the operator. Operations such as cutting quite complex interlocking curves can be challenging on a bandsaw, even though it is designed for that, so the planning and marking out – and attention to making escape cuts – are the keys to achieving the intended quality of result. Although the very nature of bandsaw construction makes certain operations challenging, with ingenuity it can make tasks easier, too. The creative aspect of bandsawing – and the speed and ease of creating a pleasing result once a method for achieving it has been worked out – can be very satisfying.

Complex curves

Freehand sawing, which the bandsaw is so eminently suited to, ought to be the easiest of all operations, but in practice it can become mesmerizing trying to follow a curving line and confusing when the shape hasn't been drawn out well. Add to that your standard fitted blade, which partway through the cut turns out to be too wide to go comfortably around some of the tighter radii, and the job turns out to be more challenging than might first appear, especially if you want a neat result.

Setting out lines is the first task. Often the design will be a mixture of straight and curved lines. If you have worked out the overall dimensions for the job, you can then set out the straight lines first and form the curved shapes or plain radii to meet those lines. This gives you a head start, since you now have some fixed points to work from.

ABOVE Around the workshop or garage you will find a number suitable objects for use when drawing up shapes. The flowerpot has two usable radii. In the foreground is a crudely made trammel with a bradpoint drill to 'spike' into the work and a pencil at the other end at the correct radius position, held on with tape.

If, however, the shape is all curves and depends on your aesthetic judgement, it gets more interesting. If you are copying a style of furniture, for example, then looking at existing pieces or reference books will give you guidance on size, shape and proportion. This provides a valuable starting point.

Draw the shape on paper first – or follow the professionals and draw it out on a sheet of hardboard or MDF – then cut out a template and use it to transfer the shape to the actual workpiece. To avoid creating confusing multiple lines, promptly rub out the old ones – on board you can use fine abrasive paper to delete unwanted lines, just as you do with an eraser on a sheet of paper.

Smaller regular curves can be drawn around everyday objects such as paint tins and plates, while larger ones can be achieved by making a crude trammel or beam compass. This is a wooden stick with a nail through one end and a pencil pushed through a tight, drilled hole at the correct radius position at the other end. The stick can be any length you like, so it is possible to draw a far bigger radius than with an ordinary compass.

Alternatively, use a long steel rule pressed with your hand against a couple of panel pins tapped into the workpiece, and draw around the outside of the rule. Or practise drawing curves with your own elbow as the pivot point, and your arm as the trammel. It is possible to create reasonably fluent large curves in this way.

Clean up the lines so that you have just one solid dependable line to follow when cutting.

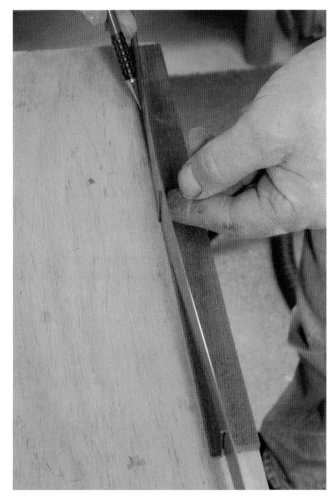

ABOVE Using a ruler and panel pins to draw a fair curve.

If there is any confusion of lines, you will end up making a last-minute decision about which one to follow and often the result is an irregular line with 'flat spots' that look bad.

The next thing to sort out is where you actually cut. It may seem obvious, but you should cut just to one side of the line, on the 'waste side' (and I do mean 'just' to one side). Unless you need some extra material – to allow for cleaning up by hand or on a drum sander, for example – you should be going for the cleanest, smoothest cut you can make. Cutting right on the centre of the line leaves no margin for error.

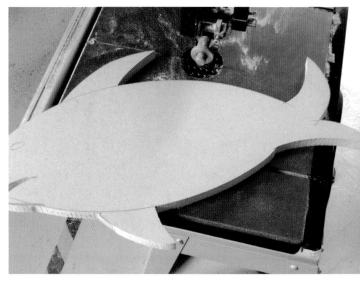

ABOVE A fish design to be given a painted finish for a children's room. Note the escape cuts already made.

ABOVE The finished result. This is not an easy shape to cut because the bandsaw column keeps getting in the way. A lot of pieces have to be removed before you can cut the finished shape.

(K)KEY POINT

Cutting into the waste is the golden rule of all woodworking activities, as it ensures that you don't undercut and mar your work. Use only fine but clear lines that you can see and follow easily.

ABOVE A tight curve like this can be attacked with a succession of close cuts, followed by sideways movement against the blade to 'nibble' the remaining wood away. It is possible to achieve quite a smooth curve with care.

Having created a satisfactory shape, check whether you need escape cuts in order to release the blade at certain points. I never like to waste good material, so I often do a fast freehand cut to slice off whole areas of board surrounding the planned cut area, and keep

ABOVE Inevitably some cleaning up and smoothing of edges will be needed. A half-round file is effective at creating a nice clean edge quickly.

them for use later on (this has the added bonus of making the workpiece more manageable, too). Always try and position the intended workpiece near the edge or corner of the material rather than in the middle, to avoid waste and simplify cutting out.

Escape cuts obviously need to be made first, and they can come up to the intended cut line at any point, allowing the waste pieces to fall away cleanly as you proceed with the final cut. Be aware that if you have to make deep escape cuts towards the middle of the board, your blade may still get trapped, even in the escape cut itself. Several smaller cuts from two different places – which free several waste pieces – may be a safer way to get to the intended deep escape cut position. The aim all the time is to try and avoid backing out of a deep cut if you can.

Cutting to the line

Although, theoretically, doing one long cut gives continuity of shape, trying to do too much in one go can cause problems, especially if you have to change hand positions. In any case, you probably have escape cut lines intersecting the line proper.

Generally it is easiest to cut away the most accessible or least difficult pieces at first, and save the more awkward scroll-type curves until last, when you can get at them more easily.

Work around the entire shape until all cuts are done. It is possible to 'nibble' with the blade at areas that don't quite follow the line. However, it may be better to clean up afterwards with a rasp, file, microplane or Surform tool instead.

Sawn veneers

If you want to do furniture restoration, or make expensive hardwoods go further, creating sawn veneers is a useful technique. You can buy 'knife-cut' veneers but they need to be ordered in quantity and often only small sections are actually required. In any case, to be 'correct', thicker sawn veneers usually need to be used when restoring antique furniture.

Make sure your bandsaw is well set up with a ⅝in (16mm) or wider sharp blade with skip teeth, as you would use for deep-cutting. Your fence should be a

> **TIP**
>
> A stock of hardboard for laying out designs and making templates is invaluable. ¼in (6mm) or thinner MDF will serve the same purpose.

high one and accurate, and the stock should already be well prepared so it runs through smoothly.

In order to cut economically and to produce veneers of the right thickness, you need to be able to measure them accurately. There is no substitute for a set of vernier or dial callipers, whether nice expensive metal ones, or the cheap plastic variety. Once you understand how to read the scale it becomes an easy and precise way to check thickness, and they can be used for many other measuring tasks around the workshop. Depending on how rigid your machine and fence are, and on the sharpness of the blade, with care you can create quite thin veneers down to about ⁵⁄₆₄in (2mm), before they start to 'feather out' and cease to be consistently thick. In any case, veneers produced in this way have blade marks that need removing by planing or sanding.

ABOVE Cutting a thick veneer: note how it curls away from the parent stock as the stresses in the timber are released. In practice this won't matter once it is glued and firmly clamped to its substrate.

The width of veneer you can produce is limited by the height under the guides. This in itself will limit the uses you can put these veneers to. You can get around this, to a certain extent, by cutting the timber down to a width that will go under the guides when turned on edge. Supposing you have a 12in (305mm) wide board, rip it to 6in (152mm), cut it into two lots of veneer, then – to get back to the original 12in (300mm) width, minus the saw kerf – rejoin on laying the veneer. Providing the grain pattern isn't too highly figured, the join shouldn't be obvious if it is carefully laid.

ABOVE Regular grain like this means it is easy to lay sawn veneers side by side without noticeable joins.

Finger joints

Sometimes called a comb joint, the finger joint isn't as strong as a dovetail joint, but it is good for things such as boxes. It has a workmanlike appearance, is relatively easy to make and has plenty of gluing surfaces to help hold it together.

The least complicated set-up is to use the standard fence, plus a stop block behind the blade to limit cut depth. Mark all the cutting positions on one component; each subsequent finger position is obtained by moving the fence across until the next mark is aligned with the blade.

Start with the finger recess nearest the fence. Position the fence so that the right-hand side of this recess is aligned with the blade. First cut the right-hand side

ABOVE Having drawn a series of evenly spaced finger joints, transfer the marks to the other matching joint component. Alternating waste areas must be marked clearly to avoid cutting out the wrong pieces.

ABOVE Although it isn't essential, it is a good idea to do the cuts for the edges of all the sockets before removing the waste.

of the recess. The waste is then removed a sliver at a time by moving the component to the right, alternately pushing it back and pushing it forward until the left side of the recess is reached. Having removed all you can in this way, you can then clean up the bottom of the recess by pushing the component sideways back to the fence. Since there is very little left to remove at this stage, it is perfectly possible to push sideways like this against the blade without difficulty. Cut the corresponding recess on each component before adjusting the fence.

Note that for a joint to assemble correctly, one half needs to be turned the other way up, so the fingers match the recesses. This fact will also affect the marking and cutting out of joints at each end of the components.

Having done the first recess on all the components, move the fence to the left until the right-hand side of the next recess is aligned with the blade and proceed as before. Continue until all the recesses are cut. At all times the rear stop block stays in the same position. It sounds complicated but is quite easy to achieve, and quick too.

ABOVE When doing the corner cut from both directions, you will be left with a tiny piece of waste blocking the area next to the blade. Always switch off to remove it.

ABOVE The other half of the joint is a similar affair as regards cutting out the sockets.

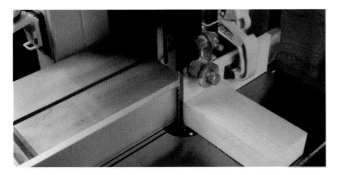

ABOVE This simple L-shaped stop jig is employed to get uniform socket depth. The fence is moved across for each cut.

ABOVE The finished joint. Note how the fingers are slightly longer than strictly necessary. They will be sanded level once all the joints are glued.

Cutting tight curves

Using a narrow scroll-cutting blade is fine if you happen to have one fitted to the bandsaw, and it is well worth changing blades for a long run of work. But what if you have just a few components to cut? In the examples shown, there are some very tight radii but a fairly wide blade.

Start by marking a series of straight escape cuts that also take in any short straight cuts in the design. Note how on a tight external radius the workpiece has to be jiggled slightly to get enough space for the blade to continue along the marked curve.

Next do all the escape cuts, then attack each arc with a series of straight lines running into the remaining waste area. Finally, run along each internal curve, twisting the workpiece just enough to persuade the rather wide blade to more or less follow the curve. Each finger of waste will then obligingly pop out of the way as you proceed to cut the rest away.

So, without the aid of a narrow blade, it has still been possible to do the impossible, so to speak: the bandsaw and blade are pushed beyond what we should reasonably expect them to do.

ABOVE Do the easy straight cuts first; these delineate the start and finish of each intended curved cut and act as escape cuts.

ABOVE Several straight cuts help the blade ease around the curve as the smaller pieces fall away.

> **TIP**
>
> Learn the 'nibbling' technique with the bandsaw by practising on some spare pieces of wood. You will discover that the bandsaw can be used almost like a rasp, working the wood sideways and backwards and forwards against the teeth to help clean up rough edges. This cannot be done with deep cuts, as it is only possible to make this brushing motion on the edges of fairly thin timber.

ABOVE When cutting an exterior curve with a wide blade, reversing the blade slightly and then widening the cut path enables the blade to cut around a tight curve, giving a neat finish.

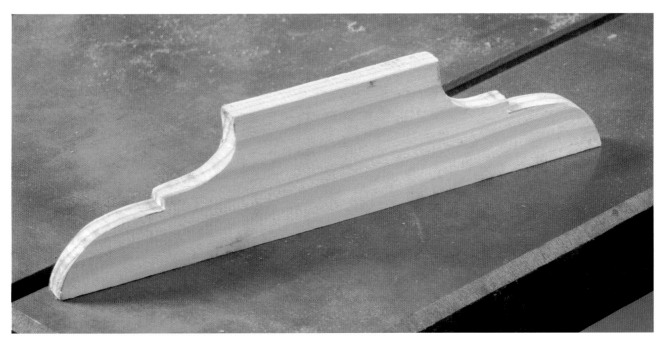

ABOVE The finished item.

Haunched mortise and tenon

The mortise and tenon is one of the oldest, strongest and most reliable of joints. It dates back to ancient Egyptian times, but is still very much with us. It is well worth looking at reference books on the subject of joints to understand the different versions of the mortise and tenon (such as *Success with Joints* by Ralph Laughton, published by GMC).

The haunched mortise and tenon is a typical version used in table and chair frames. The mortise or slot is always cut first, either using a router and jig (as shown on left), or by chopping out the slot by hand with a chisel and mallet. The haunch is a small step taken out of the tenon to match a similar step in the mortise, which reduces the chance of the wood breaking where the tenon is close to the end of a component.

Because this book is about the bandsaw, we will concentrate on cutting tenons, not the mortise. Nevertheless, here is a brief description of how a mortise is machined, as it is a critical part of the joint-making process.

What is required is a 'mortise box' and a ½in (12mm) shank router with a long straight cutter of a diameter to suit the mortise width. A mortise box is a simple U-shaped trough made of ply which is big enough to accommodate the components to be mortised. The router sits on top of the box with its fence attached.

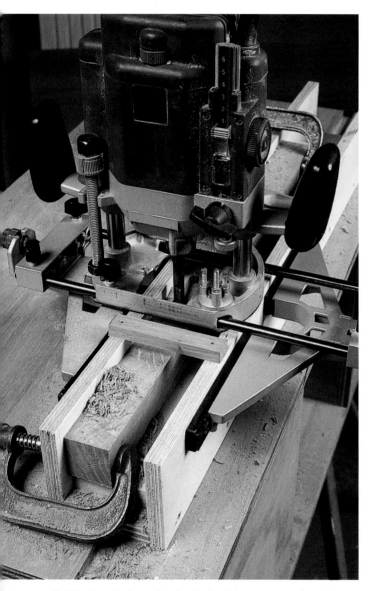

ABOVE A typical mortise box bolted down to a work surface. Note the use of two fences to stop the router wandering from side to side. The workpiece is cramped while resting on a block. There are end stops pinned on the top of the box to limit the length of the cut.

> **(KEY POINT**
>
> The mortise is normally wider than the material remaining on either side of it. There isn't a 'hard and fast' rule about this, but it is widely accepted that it is necessary in order to make the tenon strong enough to resist breakage when the joint is put under stress.

ABOVE Doing the tenon rip cut up to the marked line.

Having marked out the component, it is clamped in the mortise box which itself is clamped in a vice or screwed down to a bench surface. The router is positioned over the mortise lines and the fence adjusted so that it runs along the side of the box. This allows you to cut a neat slot with the router by eye, or to screw on a couple of end stops for the router base to press against at each end of the cut. The depth is set using the router's depth adjuster, and the depth-stop turret used to create different-depth cuts for the full mortise and for the shallower haunch at one end of the slot. This technique is described in more detail in Anthony Bailey's *Routing for Beginners*, published by GMC. A routed mortise has rounded ends and since the tenon to be cut has a small haunch, it is wise to square the ends of the mortise using a sharp, narrow chisel. This will ensure the neatest possible fit between mortise and tenon.

ABOVE Cutting the tenon shoulders; care is needed not to cut into the tenon.

129

ABOVE The first haunch cut.

ABOVE Finishing the haunch; a length stop attached to the mitre fence will ensure repeat accuracy with multiple components.

Having created an acceptable mortise, the matching tenon can be made using the bandsaw. Generally a matched set of mortise and tenon joints is required. All the mortises are cut as a batch using the same set-up, and there would normally be eight for a chair or table frame (depending on the design). Since these are identical, it is easy to set-up the bandsaw to do the eight tenons in a batch operation, one after the other.

Two main types of cut are needed – for the cheeks and the shoulders – and each tenon requires two of each. In the example shown, the shoulders have been cut first freehand, up to marked lines on the workpiece. A stop block can be used behind the blade for a more reliable result, if you wish.

Next, the shoulders are cut with the mitre fence, using the pencil lines as a guide. If the mitre fence has a length stop, that will help to produce identical-length components. You will know when to stop the forward cut, as the cheek waste will fall away, but you can fit a stop block behind the blade if required.

The last operation is cutting out the haunch, and again the straight fence and mitre fence are used. If the joint is a little tight, a sharp blade will allow you to trim the tenon slightly, or you could use a sharp chisel to pare the surfaces just enough to create a tight 'non-hammer' fit – i.e. you should not need to hit it hard to get the joint to close. Once all the joints have been made and checked you can glue up lightly, applying glue to the tenon faces, not the mortise.

Lap joints

The lap joint is easier than cutting a tenon, although the technique is the same. Each half of the joint needs to be identical in thickness, or exactly half the thickness of the wood. To achieve a good flush joint at the corner when assembled, the lap shoulder should be marked down exactly the width of the other component.

Use the rip fence for the long rip cut, and the mitre fence for the shoulder cut on both components, and you should end up with a neat, flush, corner lap joint. You can do an in-line lap in the same way to extend the length of available stock, but it will never be as strong as unjointed wood. As with tenons, you can use stop blocks for reliable repeat cutting without having to mark up all the components.

ABOVE Cutting a lap joint is very similar to cutting a tenon.

ABOVE Straight and corner lap joints are cut in exactly the same way, it is just the orientation of components that changes.

Fenced curves

Bizarrely, the straight fence will actually cut curves. How can this be? Not difficult once you think about it – for a start, we are only cutting external curves that will curve away from the fence when being machined.

Mark and cut out the first curve, using one of the methods previously described under 'Complex curves', on page 120. Now set the fence the required distance away from the blade.

Feed the timber onto the blade, and swing it gently in the direction of the curve – don't push it along the fence, or you will end up with one straight side. Hand and eye co-ordination must be used here, to end up with a parallel, smooth-curved workpiece.

This method is ideal for manmade boards, as you can produce a repeat curved section from quite a wide piece. This is not an exact technique, and the edges may need a little smoothing, but it is quite easy to do.

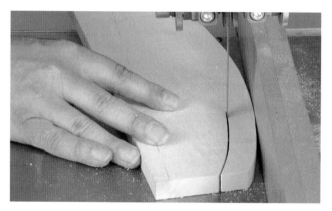

ABOVE The first cut is done accurately freehand, and the first component proper can now be cut.

RIGHT Two finished components and the waste piece.

BELOW Progressing the cut.

SAFETY TIP

As with all close freehand working, it is easy to concentrate too much on the cut at the expense of precious fingers. Push sticks are only part of the answer with a freehand job: make sure you shift your grip on the workpiece and have one hand behind the blade pulling the work through. The bandsaw cannot 'kickback' like a tablesaw, so this back hand will be quite safe, but have the blade guard fully down so your arm isn't exposed to danger.

Compound and bevel cutting

This can cover straight-line, bevel, or curved cuts, but with the table tilted. Most bandsaws have tilting tables and, while for 95 per cent of the time this might seem of no value, for those awkward jobs requiring difficult angled cutting the tilting table comes into its own: the blade stays absolutely vertical, and therefore always in the same plane to the operator's perception, a positive boon compared to the tablesaw, where the table stays fixed and the blade tilts. However, due the flexibility of cut possible with the bandsaw, a degree of mental confusion can set in.

Straight bevel cut

Try a straight bevelled cut first. Calculate what angle you want to achieve on the edge of a board and see if you can replicate it with an actual cut. Some bandsaws have protractor scales to allow accurate setting, but you may need to check that it is zeroed correctly first. If there is no scale, then a sliding bevel or a special machine-setting protractor will be needed, in order to get the exact tilt required.

It makes sense to have the straight fence set on the lower side of the tilted table, if at all possible. This will allow the workpiece to rest on the fence by gravity, while you feed it through the blade. Not all bandsaws have such an adaptable fence: often they will only work to the left of the blade, but clamping a board on instead is a makeshift option.

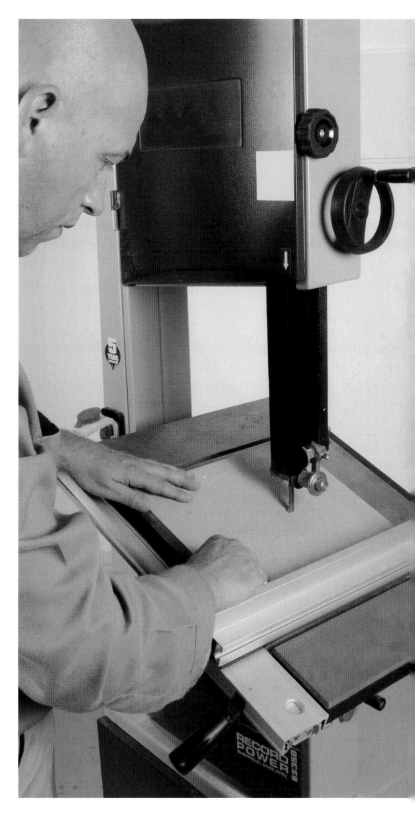

RIGHT Having the fence on the lower side of the table allows gravity to help when pushing through a straight cut.

Compound bevels

Compound bevel cutting is more complicated, as it involves forming mitres or bevels in two planes. Creating just one or two successive joints is a bit easier than making a complete frame.

It is essential to do test cuts, perhaps using stock that is well overlength, so that you can afford to waste some. In theory, the protractor on the trunnion under the table, plus the protractor on the mitre gauge, should give you accurate combined readings before cutting, but you cannot rely on this.

The problem with setting out and cutting mitres is what might be termed 'mitre blindness', that is confusing one angle for the other. Everyone who has ever cut mitres has made this mistake, usually being left with components that have the wrong angle at one end and are too short. However, with a bit of experimentation on test pieces you will arrive at the desired result and it is definitely worth persevering to get it right.

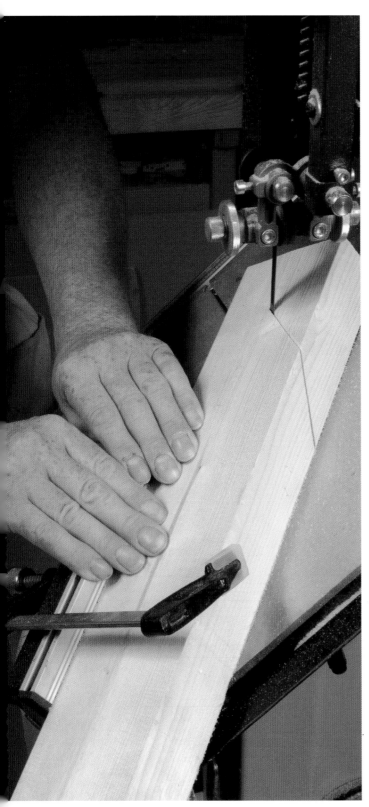

ABOVE The guard needs to be raised higher than usual to clear the workpiece, and a clamp is essential.

ABOVE It is quite difficult getting both angles just right, so test pieces are vital if you are to achieve an acceptable result.

Compound curves

The one big advantage here is that you are not generally trying to match joints as you would with a compound bevel or mitre. There is much more scope for creative freedom when cutting curves on the tilt. Indeed, you may have to accept some degree of latitude in the final result compared to the initial design. In any case, what may look fine in two dimensions on paper will inevitably look different when transferred to three dimensions.

It is perfectly possible to do 'mirror' cutting, where you have two matching but opposite components that will be seen in close conjunction and therefore need to be – to all intents and purposes – completely identical. To make this work, you will need a template for marking out that can be turned over to mark on the other workpiece. Some models allow you to tilt the table backwards towards the case and, because of the blade action, this may make it easier to achieve a true mirror image.

ABOVE When the workpiece is fed at an angle to the blade, it can be harder to visualize the resulting shape.

ABOVE Cutting more or less in line with the table should not be too challenging.

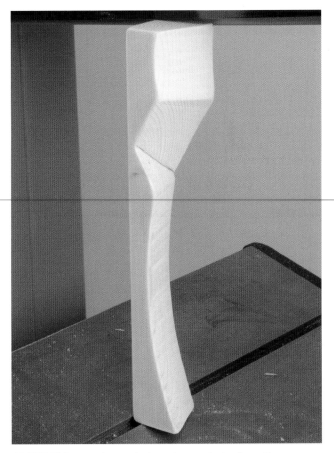

ABOVE This experimental piece demonstrates how the curves can alter unexpectedly during cutting.

(i) KEY POINT

When tilted, some bandsaw tables go 'out of true' – they are not perpendicular to the case when viewed from the side of the blade towards the case column. Check this is not so with your machine. If it does occur, it may be possible to twist the table gently on its trunnions before locking it at the desired angle.

Deep-cutting

A narrow board, in particular, will need to be planed straight and square before attempting deep-cutting, otherwise the blade will run off course. It is sensible to have a high fence (see page 157), but it is possible to make do with the standard one. The key is not only to have a sharp, well-tensioned blade, but one which is reasonably wide – at least ½in (12m) – with only a few skip teeth per inch in order to clear the waste quickly. Even more than usual, the set-up of the guides is critical to success. The fence will have been adjusted to give a parallel cut, as described on page 59. Do not force the pace of cut – let the blade take care of it. The result should be good, clean, parallel boards that just need dressing on a planer.

LEFT A firm grip is needed to ensure the board doesn't move away from the fence and allow the cut to wander.

BELOW LEFT A push stick is useful when the blade reaches the back end of the board.

BELOW The result in this case is two boards with an attractive figure, which could be book-matched together to give a mirror-image effect, perhaps for a door panel.

Freehand resawing

Resawing has been mentioned on page 114. There, a straight fence was used, but it is perfectly possible to work without a fence. Why would we want to do this? Suppose you have a rather irregular baulk of timber with a straight pencil line that you have just drawn down the middle. There is no way that timber with very uneven faces will sit neatly against a fence, even though the edge sitting on the table may be reasonably flat.

Make sure you have a sharp, wide, skip-tooth blade fitted, and some wedges handy in case the cut closes up on the blade. This is one of those few occasions where it is easier to cut on the line rather than just off to one side. The cut may not be particularly accurate – the purpose is simply to cut rough timber into one or more usable planks. This method is very useful if your bandsaw has a 'lead' and the blade cuts at a slight angle, since there is no fence-following to worry about.

KEY POINT

Frequently, timber that is divided by sawing will change shape – sometimes quite seriously – because the stresses in the wood are released when cut. Often the outside of the timber is dry, yet it is still wet in the middle – especially if it is very thick timber – because it takes much longer for it to dry inside. While resawing is a valuable technique, for stable, critical applications it can make more sense to build up timber thickness from thinner, drier sections glued together.

KEY POINT

This technique won't work well if you attempt it with very narrow stock, because you cannot rely on it sitting dead upright on the table as the cut proceeds.

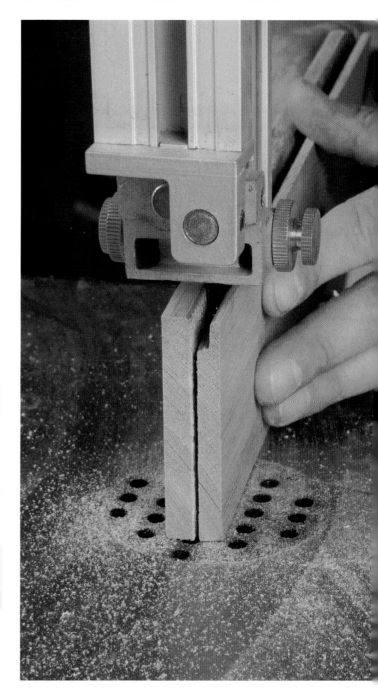

RIGHT Here a piece of prepared timber with a groove is being resawn, using the edge of the groove as a convenient cut guide. Normally a gauge-marked line would be used instead.

Circle cutting

Some bandsaws have a circle-cutting attachment as an optional extra, which is generally a metal arm that bolts onto the bandsaw case near to the blade column. This allows you to cut circles out of solid wood or ply, which can be very useful for wooden toys, decorative items and the like.

First, make a straight cut in the workpiece, to a point where it will be possible to cut out the entire circle with a bit of waste around it. Then push the adjustable steel point on the metal arm into the centre of your intended circle. Within the attachment's limits, the radius can be changed to suit the job.

> **TIP**
>
> Cut the workpiece square and slightly oversize at first, to make it more manageable.

ABOVE It is important to ensure the tip of the rod is pushed firmly into the board to be cut. Note the straight cut level with the blade, made before circle-cutting can begin.

LEFT The cut progressing.

BELOW The finishing cut, a very quick, easy process.

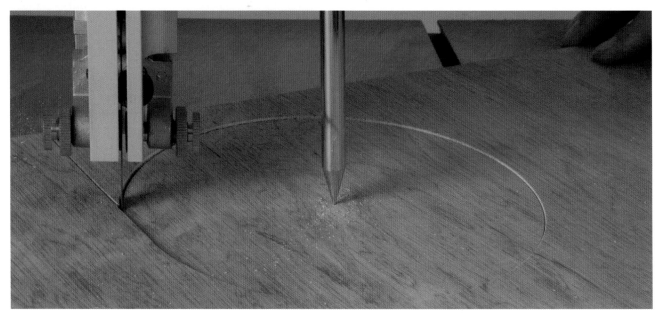

Pack cutting

This is a useful technique for cutting matching components in thin ply or MDF.

First, cut out a template and transfer to the top one of a pack of equal-sized blanks. Remove the template and, to hold the stack together, tape around the edges, or put double-sided tape between the blanks, so they will stay together.

Carefully guide the pack onto the blade, making each of the required cuts until the design is finished. Gently pull the components apart and remove the tape. You now have a pile of identical pieces.

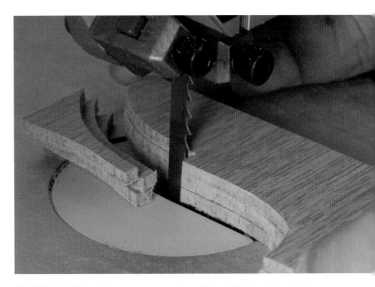

ABOVE Sticking the components together with double-sided tape will ensure no movement between the individual pieces.

ABOVE The template and the pack of blanks.

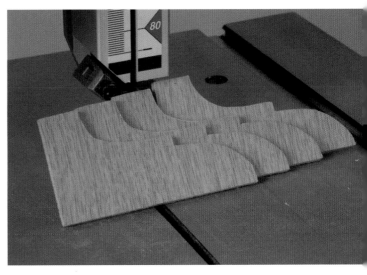

ABOVE The finished pack of identical pieces.

ABOVE Always mark with a sharp point to get an accurate line.

SAFETY NOTE

Pack cutting will produce even more small waste pieces than usual. Do not be tempted to remove them while the bandsaw is running, except with a push stick, and even then flick them away from the blade, not towards it.

Techniques for woodturners

Tapered blanks

The bandsaw is a natural machine for preparing turning blanks, and all turners who produce their own blanks have a bandsaw to hand for converting boards and rough lumps of raw timber into something usable that can be mounted on the lathe. There is no need to use a circle-cutting attachment for this and indeed I don't think anyone does – just drawing a circle on the top surface is enough to guide the cut. A neat way to get a tapered shape is to tilt the table and cut freehand so your blank already has an agreeable taper before you start turning. Mount the blank on the headstock faceplate as usual.

ABOVE Angle the bandsaw table to match the line drawn on the end of the blank.

ABOVE Advancing the cut is remarkably easy, so long as the blade is sharp and narrow enough to follow the curve.

Layered blanks

A number of different timber species can be layered either vertically or horizontally. The vertical idea is possibly safer, as the wood will hold together when subject to the stresses of turning – although turners use both methods, depending on what sort of design is wanted. Once all the surfaces are properly glued up together and dry, the normal blank shape can be cut on the bandsaw.

ABOVE The assembled blank, with vertical contrasting timber strips.

ABOVE The finished blank ready to mount and turn. Gluing and cramping must be done carefully, to avoid the blank breaking up when being turned.

Rounded tenons

Although chiselling a mortise square after cutting it using a router and mortise box is the favoured method, it is possible to bevel the tenon corners instead, thus giving a pretty good working fit in the joint. To do this you need to tilt the table and, if possible, fit the fence on the lower side of the blade. With careful set-up it is possible to trim the tenon on all four corners without any special jig, apart from a length stop clamped to the fence.

ABOVE Two opposing corners are cut with the component vertical, the other two are cut lying flat on the table.

ABOVE Cutting the waste pieces away.

ABOVE The finished tenon is not strictly rounded, but it will be a much better fit in a mortise with rounded ends than a square tenon.

Part 3:
Jigs, Templates and Devices

3:1 Push sticks and push blocks

When working around the blades of your bandsaw, tablesaw or router table, a slip could mean disaster. Push sticks and push blocks are intended to take this danger away from your fingers, as they allow you to rip and shape smaller pieces of stock with a greater level of safety. There are a number of commercial push sticks and push blocks available, but it is just as easy to make one. The design is a matter of personal taste; it is just cut from a single piece of wood and the edges rounded for comfort. A key part is the 'bird's-mouth' for standard push sticks, or a rectangular cutaway for the thin 'long-nose' type.

There is not just one ideal shape or size – this varies from woodworker to woodworker, machine to machine, and application to application – but there are three basic designs that you can customize to meet your needs. You can make your push sticks and blocks from straight, clean hardwood. Plywood or MDF are other good options, since they are less likely to split, warp or crack – but always round off any handles to prevent splinters.

The push stick is useful for feeding narrow stock between the blade and the fence. It allows you to apply a great deal of downward and forward pressure.

LEFT The design of a push stick can vary, but it needs to be comfortable to hold and should have a 'bird's mouth' notch at the end that contacts the work. Note how the bottom part has been trimmed back, so that thinner boards can be gripped properly.

(FOCUS ON:

Jigs and templates

While many bandsaw operations can be carried out with little or no use of cutting aids, there is no doubt that critical or complex operations such as dovetailing would not be possible without the aid of an appropriate jig or two. Indeed, repetitious operations where multiple finished components are required cannot be achieved successfully without jigs and templates. Time spent building a jig or making a template is seldom wasted, and once made it can be retained for future use if the same need arises again. Many woodworkers derive almost as much satisfaction from creating effective working jigs as they do from the finished product which these devices help to make.

The flat push stick

The flat push stick is used to apply greater downward pressure on wider stock, and with its long nose there is more control over the length of the workpiece. The example shown below is quite slim and will therefore easily pass between the fence and the blade when there is limited opening. Here it is being used to press the workpiece sideways, in order to create sawn veneers. If the blade accidentally trims the step on the push stick it isn't a disaster – it will need just need reshaping.

ABOVE This long-nosed flat push stick works equally well, whether used on top or at the side of a workpiece.

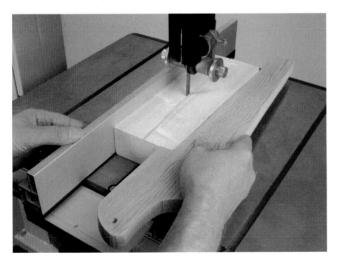

ABOVE A thicker version which is better if you are working with heavier stock.

Push block

The push block is ideal for shaping or jointing applications, as it allows you to apply a great deal of downward and forward pressure. You can make your own quite easily. It needs a fixed lip big enough to catch the edge of the wood firmly, and it is a good idea to line the underside with a piece of thin rubber material to give plenty of grip.

Note that the push block shown below will do the horizontal operation. To make vertical cuts you need one with the side piece on the other side, so that it will sit properly on the face of a vertical board.

ABOVE The handle design for this push block is borrowed from the shape of a hand plane.

ABOVE The strips are glued and pinned to the top board. The side strip can be glued along the other edge to suit vertical cuts.

3:2 Stopped cuts

The bandsaw is an ideal machine for stopped working, where the progress of the workpiece is halted by a suitable block or stop behind the blade. Stopped working produces a very precise length of cut that can be used for repetition work, for example notching out shelf corners for frame-and-panel cabinets.

Fit a wide blade and use the fence to gauge the width, and a clamped-on backstop to limit the depth of cut. Generally bandsaw tables have open castings underneath and are not made for the convenience of clamping, so use a square of ply or a batten to span some of the ribs, to create a flat clamping surface underneath.

If you are making a number of shelves, make all the cuts in one direction at one go, then turn all the shelves over to do the other meeting cuts. A feature of bandsaws compared to tablesaws is that they don't cause the grain to tear out, so turning a workpiece over and cutting from the other side is not detrimental in any way. As an alternative you can make a one-piece L-shaped fence clamped on the table instead of two separate aids.

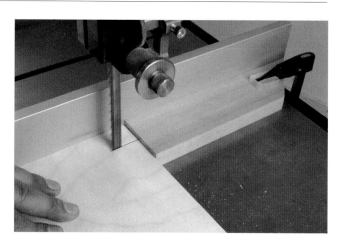

ABOVE Creating stopped cuts couldn't be easier.

> **TIP**
>
> If you make your first stopped cut near the fence and then move the fence over – for instance when joint cutting – the stop block can stay where it is. This avoids having to reset it and trying to find the same position again.

ABOVE There may be the odd occasion where it isn't practical to have the fence nearby. The stop block still works, although you need to mark any relevant cut lines to follow.

3:3 Circle-cutting jig

On page 138 we looked at using a ready-made circle-cutting jig, but you can make your own. The jig has a strip underneath to engage in the mitre slot, and a stop block which, in this case, comes to rest against a conveniently placed bolt projecting from the cast table side. It does so at a position where the screw point is level with the blade, ready to cut the circle. This jig has a complete line of holes so the screw can be adjusted towards or away from the blade to alter the actual cut diameter.

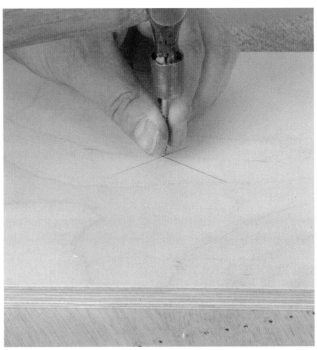

ABOVE Use a hammer and punch to make a hole for the centre screw to sit comfortably in.

LEFT The underside of the jig, showing the line of holes for the centre screw, the mitre-gauge slot strip and the stop block.

ABOVE The stop block pressing against a bolt. If your bandsaw table lacks such a convenient means, you can make a more suitable adaptation to the jig which has the same result.

3:3 Circle-cutting jig

The workpiece is pressed onto the screw point and the jig with the blank mounted on it is fed into the bandsaw by moving the slide up to the end stop. This aligns the screw point with the blade, and the workpiece is then simply rotated on the screw point.

Workpieces should be cut oversize. Using workpieces which are sized to the final diameter results in an uneven and irregular cut where the blade runs in and out of the workpiece. Using a similar concept, a jig can be made for rounding the corners of boards or frames.

ABOVE Making the first part of the cut.

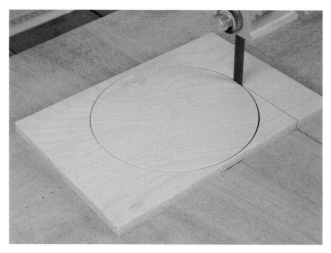

ABOVE The completed circle.

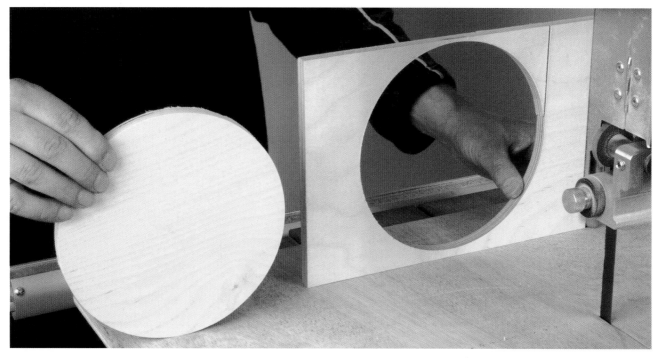

ABOVE The finished result is extremely neat.

3:4 Arc-cutting jig

There are a number of ways to cut arcs, but this one is very simple: create an original arc template, then take a squared blank (in fact a rectangular piece) and, having set an appropriate gap between blade and template, cramp the template to the table at both ends. Next, push the blank along the template so the corners touch at both ends. What should result is a curve created from a square piece moving against a curved one. It seems strange, but it does work as long as the radius isn't a tight one.

ABOVE The start of the cut.

ABOVE The cut almost finished.

ABOVE The cut has successfully separated to give an arc.

3:5 Point fence

The point fence is a simple but very underrated device, consisting of a wooden bar with a rounded point at the end. It is used in place of a standard fence to cut curves or straight sections, although the latter need to be carefully marked in order to give you a line to follow. It solves the problem of blade 'lead' with a straight fence.

The most effective use is for curved work, because it allows any shape to be produced as a parallel profile. For this, cut a suitable piece of wood to length, and shape the end so the workpiece will slide easily against it. Clamp it to the table firmly, so it cannot move at all, then run the workpiece against the point, following the line you have marked on it.

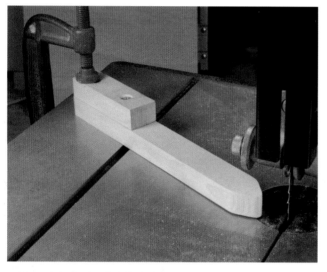

ABOVE A typical point clamped in position.

ABOVE So far it looks like a regular curve.

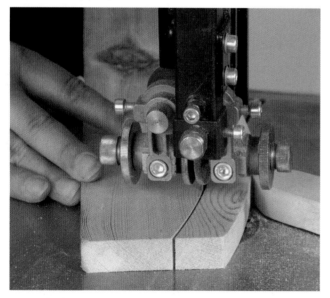

ABOVE Starting the cut.

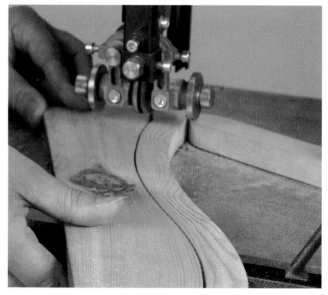

ABOVE But no! This time we have produced a lazy S-shape, something only a point fence can do.

3:6 Mitre jig

This jig uses a sheet of ⅜in (9.5mm) ply with a register strip fixed to the underside, like the circle-cutting jig described earlier. On the top side are two bevelled blocks opposing each other, to which the workpieces are clamped.

The position of the blocks for normal mitre-framing work is at 45° to the edge of the board, as is the angle of the bevel cut on the ends. In order to get the angles and positions of the jig components correct, you need to use one edge of the board as a datum, from which all measurements – both on top and underneath – are made. The blocks don't need their ends bevelled before fixing them on, as the jig, when pushed onto the blade, will trim the ends automatically to length and to the correct angle.

You could, of course, make a jig for a different set of angles just as easily. Although G-clamps may just be able to hold the workpiece in place, the recommended type would be toggle clamps: these are screwed on, can then be clamped and released quickly, and will hold anything within the designed capacity of the jig.

ABOVE The mitre-guide strip on the underside.

ABOVE Making a mitre cut. Note the use of a small block to get the correct packing thickness and avoid any marking.

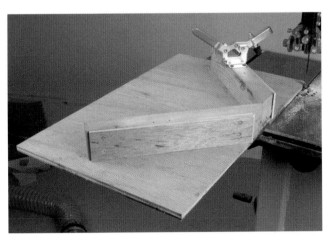

ABOVE The basic jig with just one toggle clamp in position (two might be better).

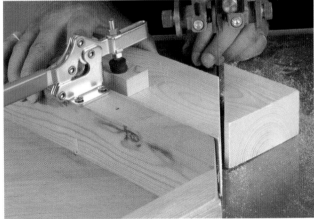

ABOVE The cut finished. It would be possible to cut two components at opposite angles at the same time.

3:7 Taper jig

Cutting repeat taper shapes can be tedious and inaccurate without a jig. The jig can be made to suit whatever tapered shapes you want. The one shown here has several steps at the back end, so that – by repositioning the workpiece – different taper angles can be produced with just one jig.

You need a decent handle for safety, and the straight fence for the jig to work against. Having cut the first taper, turn the workpiece over and make the second cut. It should be added that jigs are at their most productive when they are being used to create a whole batch of components using a jig such as this.

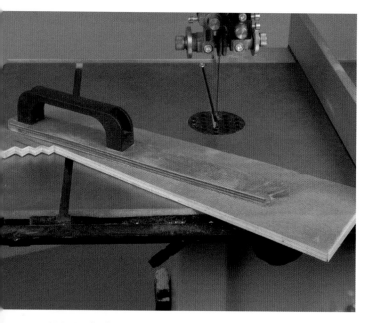

ABOVE The basic jig. Note the stops shown on the left.

ABOVE Turn the workpiece over for each successive cut.

ABOVE Making the first cut. The handle of the jig is positioned to keep the hand well away from the blade.

ABOVE A finished group of components, all cut accurately to the same taper, by means of the jig.

3:8 Template sawing

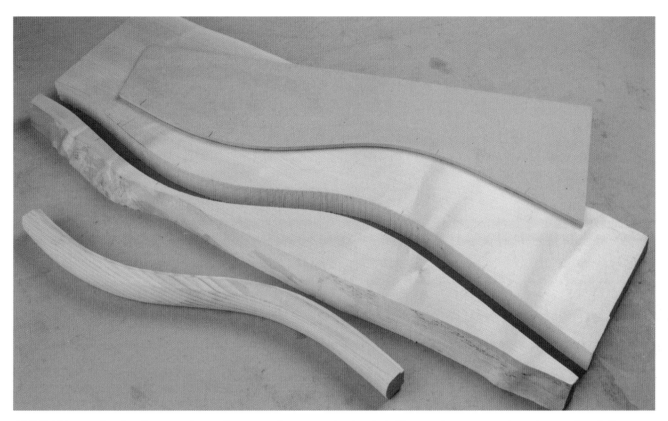

ABOVE This template has been used to make an arm for a very slender chair. The template can run along the template follower which is sited around the sawblade.

The fastest way to reproduce identical parts is with a machine guided by a template. Most woodworkers are familiar with this technique, as it applies to a router: a bearing, which is fastened to the end of a router bit, runs around the edge of a template fastened to the workpiece. The template is then fastened to the next workpiece, and the process is repeated. All pieces, whether there are 6 or 600, are exact copies, because the same template is used to guide the router.

This concept can be applied to a bandsaw for reproducing curves. Rather than drawing the design on the stock and carefully sawing to the line, a template is attached to the stock, and the cut is guided by a follow point that is secured to the table adjacent to the blade. This permits you to saw faster: instead of having to follow the layout line, you simply push the stock past the blade while maintaining contact between the template and the guide.

KEY POINT

Use good-quality ply or MDF for the template. Cheap plywood isn't suitable, because often it isn't dead flat, and it has voids in the core between the veneer layers. Because it doesn't run smoothly, the guide catches in the voids and spoils the workpiece.

3:8 Template sawing

Bandsawing with a template is definitely a fast way to produce any number of curved parts. But the technique does have a major shortcoming: you can't saw tight inside corners. In fact, the technique is most beneficial for bandsawing large, sweeping curves such as chair rockers or swept, full-height back legs.

Because making an accurate template may consume a considerable amount of time, the benefit gained by sawing with a template may not outweigh that effort. Nevertheless, bandsawing with a template can be a quick, accurate method for producing large quantities of certain types of work – in other words it is ideal for batch production rather than very small quantities.

A template is a pattern: simply draw the design and carefully cut it out – it is that simple, but it is also important to sand and generally smooth away any irregularities. If you don't take the time to do this, any faults will be replicated in the work for which the template is used.

The guide or follow point extends from the blade of the bandsaw to the edge of the table. The blade end of the follow point is notched to fit around the blade, and is convex in shape to follow the curves of the template easily. The other end is firmly clamped to the table.

KEY POINT

Once setup, the actual sawing becomes the easiest part of the job. While you're sawing, always keep the template positioned firmly against the guide.

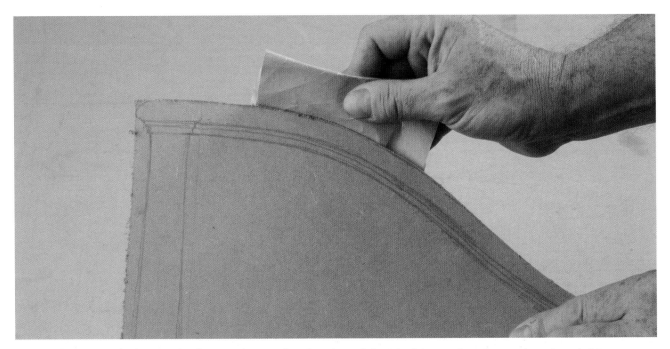

ABOVE If you want the best result, always make sure that the edges of the template are shaped properly and sanded to remove any unevenness.

Securing a template

You can attach a template to your workpiece in a number of ways. My favourite method is to fix the template to the stock with small panel pins. If you allow the heads to protrude slightly, it's much easier to pull the panel pins out again. Obviously, you don't want to use pins if the holes will show in the finished work, but usually you can position them in areas where they won't be seen, or where the offending holes in the stock will later be removed during construction. Alternatively, a spot of fine woodstopping will fill the holes.

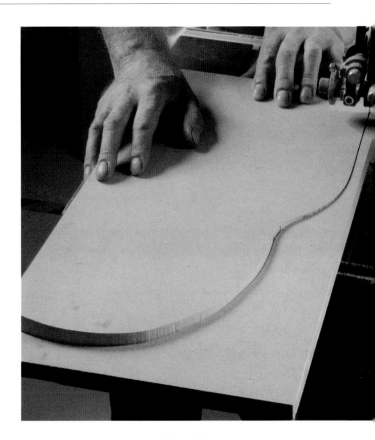

RIGHT The workpiece is fixed on top of the template. Maintaining pressure is important, as is turning the workpiece so that the blade is always more or less parallel with the surface that is being copied.

BELOW The underneath, showing the template which is actually slightly smaller than the workpiece.

3:8 Template sawing

A second option for securing a template to a workpiece is to use double-sided tape. A third option is to construct a jig that includes the template profile, plus toggle clamps to secure the work.

Toggle clamps are quick to operate and are ideal for most jig-clamping situations. Because constructing the jig takes time, I would reserve this last method for parts that are regularly reproduced.

KEY POINT

Make the template longer than the stock by ½in (12mm) or more, so that the template contacts the guide point before the work reaches the blade. This ensures a safe and precise start to the cut.

LEFT The follow point, in which the blade has been allowed to make a slot. The follow point has been carefully clamped and braced so it cannot possibly move around.

BELOW A simple but effective set-up. Two clamps may prove necessary if the follow point tends to move when the workpiece is pushed against it.

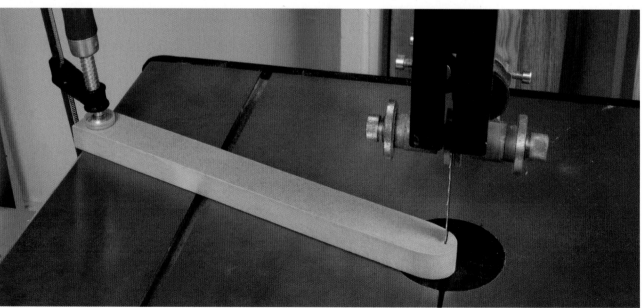

3:9 High fence

When resawing on the bandsaw you really need a high fence. This design will suit the purpose. The design and construction are quite simple and it is very rigid. Needless to say, it must sit perfectly upright on the table surface, and it can then be clamped – possibly directly to the existing fence – in any position, as required. A good-quality ply glued and pinned together will make a fence that should last for years.

We discussed fence set-up on pages 59–60 – here is a more comprehensive guide, for resaw work.

Take a piece of large-section scrap wood 2–3ft (600–900mm) long, plane a straight edge, and mark a line parallel to that edge. Rip freehand along the line, adjusting your feed direction until you are cutting consistently straight down the line.

When you have split the line for 4–5in (100–125mm), stop, hold the stock still on the table and switch off the saw. Mark a pencil line (which can be erased later) on the saw table along the straight edge of the test piece, then set your rip fence parallel to the pencil line. This is a first approximation – now you are ready for fine-tuning.

ABOVE **A firm grip and concentration are required.**

ABOVE **The high fence complete and clamped to the table ready to cut.**

ABOVE **Two boards out of one.**

3:9 High fence

Make a short resaw cut, either in the work at hand, or in a scrap piece of similar hardness and roughly similar width. With the cut completed, stand a straightedge against the resawn face of the board. Unless you are very lucky, you'll see that the blade bowed left or right within the stock. The way the blade bows tells you how to fine-tune your fence for very precise resawing. You know that the solid body of a blade cannot simply move sideways through solid wood. To create a bowed cut, the teeth must lead to one side or another within the wood (where they're free of the lateral guides' constraint), twisting the blade.

If the blade bowed to the left, adjust the rear of your fence slightly to the right, and vice versa. Make another test cut and check the face of the wood again. It may take three or four tests to get the fence set for flawless sawing, but once that's done you can resaw piece after identical piece, with cuts so straight that one pass through the planer is all it takes to produce clean, flat wood at your target thickness.

All the foregoing assumes, of course, that you are using a decent-quality bandsaw that has been setup properly. Don't expect perfect results from an imperfect machine.

ABOVE Just for comparison, an industrial resaw with an enormous 4in (100mm) wide blade and powered roller feed.

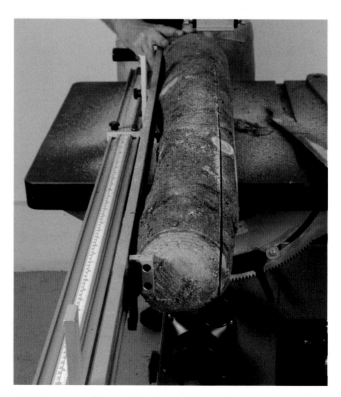

ABOVE A manufactured jig that is designed to deal with timber 'in the log'.

KEY POINT

Feeding too slowly will cut the wood adequately, but it will wear out the blade a lot faster than necessary, while if you feed too fast, the completed cut will show pronounced bands of wide, diagonal tooth marks. Practise feeding at a moderate, consistent pace, just slow enough to leave a smooth surface.

3:10 Cutting round stock

ABOVE Making a V-block is quick and easy, and it makes round work safe and efficient.

If you have ever tried to cut round-section stock on a tablesaw or bandsaw, whether dowel or a larger size, you will know what a dangerously unnerving experience it can be. Even handsawing can be very difficult, for the obvious reason that the wood won't lie still. What is worse, it will rotate in the direction the blade pulls it, thus making it a very dangerous and inaccurate way of cutting.

The solution is to make a V-block. The V-block is not only used in woodworking, but a machined cast-iron version is used in engineering for the same reason, to ensure non-rotational stability. A V-block can be made on the bandsaw as follows:

ABOVE Trimming down an old chair component.

3:10 Cutting round stock

Cut a piece of planed 3 x 2in (76 x 50mm) softwood squarely to length using the mitre gauge. Mark the V-shape on both ends, then stand it on end and cut out the 'V', making two cuts. Hold the workpiece low down for safety, taking care to hold the back faces without fingers curled around the front. In theory, if the wood is cut square at the ends, the blade should run through neatly from one set of marks to the other. In practice it will probably be slightly adrift, but if it isn't much different it shouldn't matter. Your V-block is now ready to use.

Place the round section into it and then cut to length. If the cut needs to be perfectly square, use it in conjunction with the mitre fence and push it onto the blade.

An alternative, which is useful for dealing with larger sections, is a large wedge section with the support face cut at 45°. This is held using your fingers, while the palm and thumb of the other hand grip the round workpiece. This does the same job, but needs a firmer grip to use it.

ABOVE When cutting larger round sections, such as this pear log destined for a woodturner's lathe, a more practical option is a wedge cut on the bandsaw, bisecting a large square section at 45°. Providing it and the stock are held firmly, it is a safe way to prevent the stock rolling over when being cut.

3:11 Plastic templates

Although drawing directly on wood, or making a paper template and sticking it onto the wood is easy enough, a plastic template has the advantage of allowing you to position it so that you can see where the wood grain lies. This is especially helpful in more exotic or unusual timbers with complex grain and interesting figure patterns. You can get either Perspex, which is tough and a decent thickness, or standard polycarbonate as sold for secondary glazing. The latter is thinner and sometimes inclined to shatter, but is a cheaper and more easily available alternative.

To cut thin plastic on the bandsaw you are better off with a skip-tooth blade, say 6 or 8tpi, because a fine blade intended for ply or metal is likely to clog and heat up, causing the plastic to stick to it. In the case of polycarbonate, in particular, it is necessary to ensure proper work support around the blade so the plastic can't break. It is possible to cut some quite complex shapes in a plastic template, but the more you concentrate blade activity in a small area, the more the plastic may heat and stick to the blade. Use the same technique of preparing escape cuts as you do for wood. Once the sawing is finished, a selection of files will be needed to get a truly clean shape. Any roughness on the top and bottom edges, will need to be smoothed off. These templates are not fixed to the job, but merely drawn around. The beauty of decent templates like this is that they can be saved and reused later on.

LEFT The centrepiece for a batch-produced mobile is drawn in felt-tip on the polycarbonate sheet. The features are included to make it easier to visualize the design; in practice they will be painted on afterwards.

BELOW Cutting out the template. Escape cuts are used, as for wood, to enable the blade to negotiate the curves safely.

ABOVE Ready to mark the design out. It is easy to see the grain and move the template accordingly, to find the best figure and grain direction.

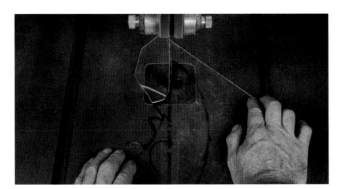

KEY POINT

A finished shape is only as good as the template that created it. The better and more carefully you make and shape your template, the better the result you will get from it.

3:12 Swinging arc jig

Cutting large regular curves more precisely than freehand can be stymied by the lack of a large bandsaw table. All bandsaws have relatively compact tables which vary in size only in relation to the overall capacity of the machine. Making jigs and sub-tables for different purposes helps to mitigate this shortcoming. In this case we are concerned with an arc that will take the pivot point well beyond the table limit. The actual workpieces it can hold are not that wide – it is the diameter of the arc which is important here.

Cut a rigid piece of board such as ¾in (19mm) ply to size. You will need a slot on the column end of the board, wide enough for the blade to move in so it can be mounted on the table. Clamp the board onto the table, overhanging on the opposite side to the column. A wooden support will be needed under the overhanging end to keep it safe and level. Next cut out a 'pie-slice'-shaped piece of thinner board for the moving part. Mark the radius you require, and drill a hole near the end of the board (or a series of jigs if you want your jig to be adjustable) and an identical hole in the baseboard near the outer end in the middle. Use a nut and bolt with washers to locate the swinging board to the baseboard. A narrow board is fixed across the swinging piece towards the blade

end, with two toggle clamps to hold the workpiece firmly. Depending on the material thickness, you may need to fix a batten first and mount the clamps on the batten. Now clamp the workpiece on the jig and push towards the blade. The result is a neat, clean arc cut, and it is easy to produce as many as required.

ABOVE A typical toggle clamp – two are required. Thicker workpieces entail mounting the clamps on a crosswise batten fixed to the jig.

ABOVE Operating the jig is extremely easy: just push the workpiece onto the blade for a very quick, precise result.

ABOVE The finished jig, ready to operate. Clamp the workpiece on, then simply swing the jig to get a neat, accurate, curved cut.

> ### Ⓚ KEY POINT
>
> A good selection of nuts, bolts, washers and adhesives like epoxy resin and superglue are essential around the workshop. There are always minor repairs, jig making, and so on, that require these. Old imperial nuts and bolts still have a place when working on older machines, but in general sizes are almost universally metric.

3:13 Dovetails

The dovetail is part of woodworking lore. It is the ultimate prize in jointmaking, requiring more skill than other forms of joint and capable of great strength and – in many cases – elegance. This is quite a lot to ask of a simple joint, and that is where the problem lies. The joint is simple to achieve in theory, but more skill is needed in practice, starting with correct setting out.

Here is a way of making a standard common dovetail joint on the bandsaw. Typically, this would be used for drawers for a chest, for instance. First, your stock must be precisely finished to size. That is to say, both faces and edges should be parallel and flat, and also square to each other. A planer-thicknesser is required to get this degree of accuracy, or very careful hand-planing.

Ensure that you have plenty of spare stock to start with, as there are bound to be some mistakes and you will need to make test joints. Cut the components to length and mark them up in sets to avoid confusion: two sides and a back and front. If you make a simple drawer box, a separate front can be added later (traditionally the front would be integral, but this does not lend itself to being cut on the bandsaw). Because the joints will run fully from corner to corner all round, all the components in their matched pairs – front and back and two sides, will be full length, with no other allowances required.

ABOVE A simple but effective jig like this will save hours of sweat and frustration with accurate marking out.

A dovetail joint consists of two distinctly different halves – the tails and the pins – which must lock together accurately for the joint to work. A simple dovetail jig such as the one shown will make the process vastly simpler, if you use the instructions that accompany it as your guide.

Each jig is different, so we will not cover the setting out in any detail, except to mention that we are creating a 'common through dovetail'. 'Common' dovetails are as wide as they are high, more or less, and the pins that lock into them are reasonably wide. 'Through' dovetails go right to the corners and are not 'blind' (hidden) behind a thin layer of wood, as is the case with integral drawer fronts, where the joint must not be visible when the drawer is closed.

There are many different kinds of dovetail joints. For more information see *Success with Joints* by Ralph Laughton, published by GMC Publications.

> **(KEY POINT**
>
> A well-made dovetail joint will stay locked together even before any glue is added – the key is accurate marking out and cutting.

3:13 Dovetails

Cutting the pins

The two outer pins always have a bit more wood to make them strong enough, and the dovetails are spaced equally in between. Once one half of the joint is marked, this can be carried over onto the other half using the jig to complete the marking process.

The pins, when viewed from the end, are in fact angled to match the dovetails. To achieve this, tilt the bandsaw table to the same angle as that of the dovetails, which for hardwood means a 1:8 slope, or in this case for softwood 1:6. In order to obtain this angle, place a marked-up component on the table, sight along, and tilt the table until the angle is identical to that marked on the component. To ensure that you know which cuts to make, pencil-hatch the waste areas, so that you don't cut into the wood you need to keep.

The problem comes when cutting the opposite slope, because the bandsaw table will not tilt the other way. What is needed is a jig that gives us the opposite tilt, and the table will be level for this. Take a wide, thick, prepared length of timber and cut it so you are left with two wedges. Note that it has been cut freehand to a line, as the blade has a distinct 'lead' that would otherwise pull the wood off course and so spoil the cut.

ABOVE Both parts of the joint (tails on the left, pins on the right) are marked out ready to cut, with waste areas clearly shown.

Place the cut side of the wedged board down on the table, with the thick edge of the board close to the blade and the fence set; trim the edge square to remove the slanted edge. Cut the wedged board to length, so it sits just in front of the blade, then fix a

reasonably high fence to it with cutouts so that it can be set close to the blade without fouling the blade guides. The fence has an L-shaped stop behind the blade, so the blade will cut just the thickness of the material. Cramp the jig in place on the bandsaw's rip fence.

LEFT and ABOVE Freehand cutting to line is easy to achieve, as long as the blade is sharp and you don't feed at too fast a rate.

ABOVE The jig components.

3:11 Dovetails

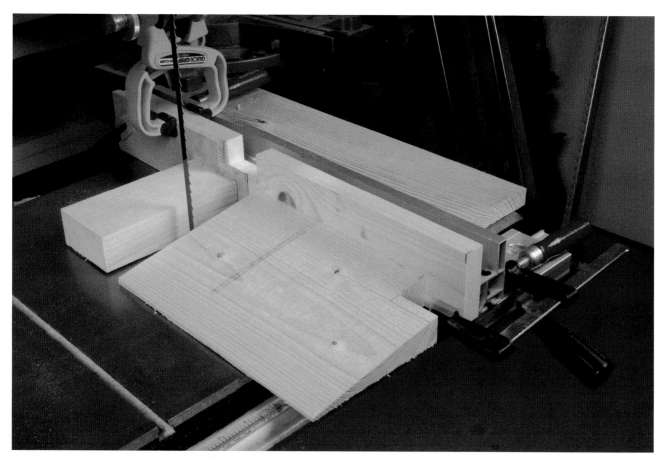

ABOVE The jig clamped in position.

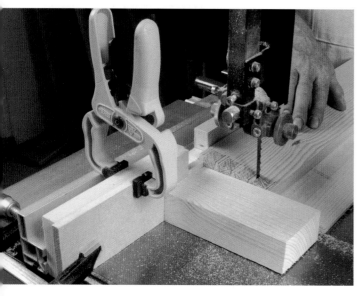

ABOVE Cutting the first pin slopes, using the wedge.

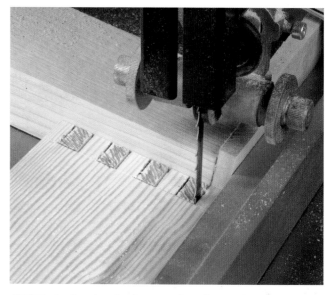

ABOVE Cutting the pin slopes at the other angle.

You can now complete the other pin slopes. To do this, remove the jig and tilt the table as described earlier, but with the L-stop clamped against the rip fence.

With the component turned upside down, so the narrower face of the pin is uppermost to avoid accidentally cutting into the pins, clean in between the sockets. Push the component onto the blade repeatedly, while moving the fence sideways slightly each time. The small remaining waste wedges can be dealt with by turning the component over the other way and again using the jig to obtain the correct angle.

Make a point of cutting all the pin slopes that are at the same angle, before making any adjustments to the set-up.

ABOVE The L-stop positioned behind the work, the blade ready to cut one set of pin slopes. Note that the table is tilted, so the pin slopes on one side are parallel with the blade.

ABOVE Careful work planning is needed to avoid any damage to the pins. The remaining waste will be removed once the workpiece is turned over.

ABOVE Using the wedge allows the remaining waste to be cut without damaging the pins. The pins are now complete.

3:13 Dovetails

Cutting the dovetails

This operation – unlike the last – is freehand apart from the stop. First, cut the dovetail slopes very carefully, by eye alone.

Next, clamp the L-stop onto the rip fence at the correct depth to match the stock thickness. Push the dovetail component on to the blade to remove the waste between the dovetails, using the L-stop to avoid cutting too deep. Once all the dovetails are cut, use a sharp bevel-edged chisel to clean the bottom of each opening between the dovetails.

ABOVE Nibbling out waste, an alternative to paring with a chisel.

ABOVE Cutting by eye and hand alone is satisfying and perfectly easy to do.

Now is the moment of truth, as you offer both parts of the joint up together. It is likely that they won't quite want to fit first time, but hopefully they will be tight, definitely not loose. To achieve a neat, tight fit, use a wider bevel-edged chisel to clean the pin slopes where necessary. Pare with the chisel sparingly, until the fit is just right and hand pressure or gentle taps with a mallet and block are enough to assemble the joint successfully. All the joint surfaces should be completely flush.

ABOVE The completed dovetails.

ABOVE A neat, strong and reliable joint.

Resources

Bandsaw manufacturers and suppliers

Axminster Power Tool Centre
www.axminster.co.uk

Craftsman
www.sears.com

Delta
www.deltamachinery.com

DeWalt
www.dewalt.com

Felder Maschinbau
www.felder-gruppe.at

Felder UK
www.ukfelder.co.uk

Grizzly Industrial
www.grizzly.com

JET
www.woodmachinery.co.uk

NMA (Agencies) Ltd
www.nmauk.com

Record Power
www.recordpower.co.uk

Ryobi
www.ryobitools.com
www.ryobipower.co.uk

Scheppach GmbH
www.scheppach.com

SIP
www.sip-group.com

Startrite
www.startrite.co.uk

Bandsaw blades

Axminster Power Tool Centre
www.axminster.co.uk

A.A. Smith Ltd
www.aasmith.co.uk

Rutlands Ltd
www.rutlands.co.uk

Scott and Sergeant
Woodworking Machinery Ltd
www.machines4wood.com

Health and Safety

National Safety Council (USA)
www.nsc.org

Health & Safety Executive (UK)
www.hse.gov.uk

For further guidance see the Health & Safety Executive code of practice booklet *Safety in the use of narrow band saws* (Woodturning Sheet No 31) on their website: www.hse.gov.uk/pubns/wis31.htm

Glossary

Air-dried timber
Timber which has been converted into board and left under cover to allow some of the natural moisture content to evaporate.

Bandwheel
A bandsaw generally has two, occasionally three of these. The steel blade is stretched over them as a 'band' – hence the name.

Bevel cut
A cut made with the bandsaw table tilted from the vertical axis. Often referred to as a mitre cut.

Blade guard
A guard for the bandsaw blade, covering that part which neither runs within the casing nor is used for actual cutting.

Box joint or finger joint
A corner joint made up of interlocking 'fingers'. Most commonly used for making boxes, hence the name.

Break-out
Torn wood fibres created by the action of the blade cutting, usually on cross-grain cuts. Generally it occurs on the side where the blade leaves the wood.

Cast iron
Molten iron that is cast in a mould to create a specific shape. The rough casting has to be machined and finished before it can be used.

Compound mitre
A mitre which is angled in two planes rather than just one, by tilting the saw table and angling the mitre fence.

Crosscut
A cut made across the grain of the wood.

Dovetail
A traditional cabinetmaking joint that is both strong and decorative. It requires skill in the execution and is still regarded as the mark of a good craftsman.

Face and edge (UK)
The two best adjoining surfaces on prepared wood, shown clearly with pencil marks.

Feed rate
The rate at which the work is moved through the saw blade. Too slow a speed can cause burning, too fast can make the blade stall.

Fence
An adjustable guide used to control the workpiece and help steer it through the saw blade.

Figure
The pattern of grain on the surface of wood, especially when it is irregular and particularly attractive. It often is revealed during resawing to create 'book-matched' boards.

Guides
The means by which the blade is controlled accurately through the wood. Normally present both above and below the table.

Heat treatment
Altering the properties of metal by subjecting it to a sequence of temperature changes (also known as tempering). Heat treatment affects properties such as strength, hardness, ductility and malleability.

High-volume low-pressure (HVLP)
A type of dust extractor best suited to machines larger than power tools. Has a large dust and chippings capacity but draws waste away at a relatively low suction pressure.

Glossary

Isolator switch
A safety device, mounted on the machine or the wall, to cut off the electrical current in an emergency or when the machine is left unattended or for maintenance.

Jig
Any kind of accessory designed to make create a precise, repeatable result. Frequently they are home-made.

Joinery (UK)
Making wood components, such as windows and doors, which are fitted to buildings.

Joinery (US)
Making any kind of furniture and fittings.

Kerf
The cut made by a saw blade. A bandsaw blade produces a much narrower kerf than a tablesaw.

Kiln-dried timber
Hardwood timber that has had its natural moisture reduced, by storage in a heated chamber, to a level which is acceptable for final use in a dry, domestic-type environment, thus ensuring stability in the wood without further shrinkage.

MDF
Medium-density fibreboard, made with compressed wood fibre and resin. Normally contains formaldehyde, which is potentially dangerous, so finished work should be sealed.

Microfilter
An electrical appliance for extracting the dangerous, minute dust particles created during cutting.

Mitre cut
An angled cut made across the face, edge or end of a workpiece.

Mitre gauge
An adjustable guide used to control and steer the workpiece as it is crosscut; adjustable to give a variety of cut angles.

Mortise and tenon
A joint that goes back to almost the dawn of carpentry as we know it; a basic and strong means of connecting timber at right angles.

Movement (in timber)
Changes in the shape or size of wood caused by water absorption or loss, and the release of internal stresses when the wood is cut. Planing after sawing corrects this problem.

No-volt-release (NVR) switch
The normal on-off switch on a machine. It must be easy to switch off quickly. If the mains supply fails, the machine cannot possibly be restarted without pressing the on button first, hence 'no-volt' release.

PAR ('Prepared All Round')
Timber that is planed on all four of its faces.

Poly-vee
A wide, flat pulley drive belt, sometimes used on bandsaws. The side that presses on the pulley wheels has a series of lengthwise V-notches, hence the name (poly is the Greek for 'many').

Push stick
An essential safety accessory held by the operator, to control the workpiece safely without danger to the operator's hands.

Resawing
The technique of sawing thick boards into thinner ones.

Rip cut
A cut made with the grain.

Sawn timber
Timber that has been cut into usable sections but not planed.

Sheet material

Ply, blockboard or other manmade board, generally available in an 8 x 4ft (2440 x 1220mm) board size. Requires no surface preparation, as such boards are manufactured to critical thickness.

Skip-tooth blade

A blade type which has become standard on bandsaws. Alternate teeth are replaced by a large gullet which allows the sawdust to escape easily, thus avoiding clogging.

Stopped working

Work in which the cutting action is limited by a block or jig, to produce repeated cuts of uniform length.

TCT

Tungsten-carbide-tipped tooling and blades are commonplace in other machines but not widely available for bandsaw blades. Only of interest to the trade.

Tension

In the context of a bandsaw the amount of 'stretch' applied to a bandsaw blade so that it is taut enough to cut safely and accurately. Different widths and thicknesses of blade require different degrees of tension.

Throat plate or table insert

A replaceable component which fills the gap between the bandsaw blade and the opening in the table through which it passes. It can be regarded as a semi-disposable item.

Thrust bearing

A device, usually a roller bearing, mounted behind the blade to limit its backwards travel. It may be fitted flat-on or edge-on, depending on the machine design.

Timber (lumber in the US)

Felled trees, partly converted or unconverted for use.

TPI (teeth per inch)

A means of identifying how fine or coarse a blade is. Fine teeth are used for thin material, coarse teeth for deep-cutting.

Trammel

A bar with a point at one end and a means of making a line at the other, used for creating circles. It needs to be adjustable and is usually home-made.

Trunnions

Semi-circular gear-toothed brackets under the table. The purpose is to support the table while allowing the angle of it to be altered.

Veneer

A thin layer of wood, generally no more than several millimetres thick.

Workpiece

A piece of wood (or other material) that is in the process of being worked, or made into something.

Index